Edmund Turney

Baptismal Harmonies

Baptismal Hymns

Edmund Turney

Baptismal Harmonies
Baptismal Hymns

ISBN/EAN: 9783337715311

Printed in Europe, USA, Canada, Australia, Japan

Cover: Foto ©Lupo / pixelio.de

More available books at **www.hansebooks.com**

BAPTISMAL HARMONIES:

OR

BAPTISMAL HYMNS,

PREPARED WITH SPECIAL REFERENCE TO THE DESIGN AND SIGNIFICANCY OF THE ORDINANCE, IN ITS RELATION TO THE WORK OF CHRIST AND THE EXPERIENCE AND PROFESSION OF HIS PEOPLE.

WITH APPROPRIATE ORIGINAL MUSIC.

By EDMUND TURNEY,

LATE PROFESSOR OF BIBLICAL LITERATURE AND INTERPRETATION IN THE FAIRMOUNT THEOLOGICAL SEMINARY.

"The statutes of the Lord are right, rejoicing the heart."—Ps. 19 : 8.

"Let the word of Christ dwell in you richly in all wisdom; teaching and admonishing one another in psalms and hymns and spiritual songs, singing with grace in your hearts to the Lord."—Col. 3 : 16.

NEW YORK:
SHELDON & COMPANY, Publishers.
1862.

Entered according to Act of Congress, in the year 1861,
By EDMUND TURNEY,
in the Clerk's office of the District Court for the Southern District of New York.

The metrical tunes, with one or two exceptions, as also the chants and anthems, embraced in this collection, are now published for the first time, and are severally covered by the copyright under which the volume is issued. The same is true of the baptismal hymns appearing in connection with the music, with the exception of three which were published in a volume of the author some years ago.

SUGGESTIONS WITH REGARD TO THE USE OF THE VOLUME.

While it is in the plan of the book to furnish an appropriate tune in immediate connection with each of the hymns, it may frequently occur, that a tune of the same metre on some other page, will be preferred. A list of all the tunes thus related respectively will be found opposite the first line of each of the hymns on page 92.

Congregations that may not at once become acquainted with the new music here published, will be aided, in their use of the volume, by a reference to the list of old familiar tunes which is given on page 94.

Several of the hymns relating to the doctrine of baptism, are not designed exclusively or chiefly for *baptismal occasions*. The most interesting and effective allusions to the import and uses of baptism, which appear in the apostolic epistles, are retrospective. And it can hardly be doubted that allusions of this kind, embodied in the hymns which are used on ordinary occasions of worship, whether public or social, would frequently answer a most valuable purpose. Has not the practice prevalent in most of our churches, of appropriating exclusively to baptismal occasions, hymns which convey any direct allusion to baptism, or to that which is symbolized in baptism, been adopted with too little regard for the natural operation of devotional feeling, in its recognition of the Scriptural incentives to Christian piety and usefulness? There seems to be no reason why hymns like that relating to the profession made in baptism on page 51, and which, with the sweet strain of music furnished for it, so well adapted for use in the social meeting, or at the fire-side, is repeated on pages 89 and 90, should be excluded from the ordinary psalmody of Christian worship. The same may be said of the hymn referring to the twofold baptism of our Savior, on page 63, of the form of chant in which is repeated the history of His baptism in the river Jordan, including the united testimony of the Father and the Spirit to His divine mission and character, on pages 77 and 78. of the pieces relating to the fullness of the Spirit's influence, on pages 83 and 73—76. as well as of others indicated on page 83. In the use of the Doxology in our churches, nothing would seem more natural or appropriate than the occasional recognition of the fact so prominently set forth in Mat. 28: 19, to wit, that the threefold name which is introduced into the expressions of praise or prayer employed by the baptized worshipper, is one which is identified with the very nature of his profession as a Christian. In most of the hymn books in common use, we look in vain for any form to express this natural relation of thought. In the three forms of address to the Father, the Son and the Holy Spirit, presented on the following pages, this association of ideas has been, not inappropriately, it is believed, preserved.

The list of hymns and other pieces adapted for use on ordinary occasions of worship, which is furnished on page 83, will, with respect to the foregoing suggestions, be found convenient for reference.

The general arrangement of the hymns of the volume, has respect partly to the relation of subject, and partly to considerations of practical impression. It will easily become familiar to one using the volume.

WARREN, Music Stereotyper, Rear 43 Centre-st. New York

PREFACE.

The general characteristic features of this little volume are stated, perhaps, with sufficient distinctness, on the title page. It is designed to answer the twofold purpose of a baptismal Hymn and Music Book, to be used in connection with devotional exercises, and of a book of instruction and persuasive appeal for more general circulation. Its title is intended to be more deeply significant of its design and character than might be obvious apart from a particular examination of its contents and its arrangement. In addition to the sweet and effective "harmonies" of musical chords embodied in the tunes respectively, the author has sought to secure a special and obvious harmony between the general sentiment and expression of each of the hymns, and the character and effectiveness of the music accompanying it; while the book, in another feature of it, is designed to render conspicuous the harmony existing between the doctrine of baptism as exhibited in the several pieces, and the authoritative teaching of the Scriptures. Nor is the least interesting and suggestive harmony which it may be found adapted to illustrate. that which exists between the exposition given of the design and symbolical import of the ordinance, and the *experience* of the Christian in his conscious fellowship with Christ, and his thankful appreciation of the great facts set forth in his profession.

It has been the aim of the author to cover the whole range of Scriptural teaching with respect to the design and significancy, and the more important doctrinal and practical and historical relations of the rite. While there is no intentional recurrence, at several points, to some of the more important aspects of baptism, and the occasional repetition of a phrase extending through a line or portion of a line, each of the hymns has been prepared with reference to its adaptation to answer a specific purpose in its relation to the whole. It is designed, not to be a general expression of thoughts more or less related to baptism, but to be conformed to some principle of unity and completeness, which, obvious to the apprehension of the author, will, it is believed, in most cases, be easily apparent to the mind of the reader.

While a few of the hymns are naturally either expostulatory or declarative in their form of expression, there has seemed to be no necessity, for any purpose, either of instruction or impression, for resorting to the didactic style.

In most of the pieces the characteristic language of devotional feeling or emotion, has been spontaneously, and in some sense necessarily adopted. While they thus embody the natural expression of Christian experience in its apprehension and practical appreciation of the great facts and truths of the gospel, they may, for this very reason, have the additional advantage of being more fully and effectively *instructive*, than might have been possible by the adoption of a more didactic style.

In variety of metre, rhythm and general form and style of poetic expression, as well as in special appropriateness for particular occasions, it is hoped they will be found adapted to the various purposes for which baptismal hymns are required.

The music accompanying the hymns has, in every instance, been furnished expressly for the words. The names of the several composers will, for the most part, be a sufficient guaranty for the general excellence of the pieces. The aim, in the preparation of the book, has been to procure music which should combine, as far as possible, the characteristics of appropriateness, sweetness and melody and animation of expression, and originality. And as most of the tunes will be found adapted for use on ordinary occasions, in the singing of hymns requiring the same general musical expression, it is believed their introduction into choirs and churches cannot fail to add very perceptibly to the interest and profit of the ordinary exercises of public and social worship. The writer indulges the persuasion that not a few whose hearts may be touched in the use of the sweet strains of music which are here supplied, will unite with him in sincere and grateful acknowledgements to the gentlemen whose names stand at the head of the several pieces, for the generosity and favor which they have shown in enabling him to realize so fully the conception in which the volume originated.

It is with him occasion for devout thankfulness, that, in the affliction which, for a season, has deprived him, for the most part, of the use of his voice in the prosecution of the more public labors of the ministry, it is within his power to make this attempt to fulfill the great commission, by "teaching" the truth of the gospel in the truly evangelical method indicated in Col. 3 : 16. If the use of the volume shall contribute, to any considerable extent, towards awakening apprehensions of the truths of the gospel which have a relation to baptism, similar to those which have aided in its preparation, its publication will not be in vain.

NEW YORK, January, 1862.

INTRODUCTORY REMARKS,

WITH SPECIAL REFERENCE TO THE IMPORTANCE OF THE TRUTH PROCLAIMED BY THE RITE.

The doctrine of baptism, in most of its aspects and relations, may be left with the brief but explicit and suggestive statement and exposition of it presented on the following pages. This remark is applicable to many of the considerations, arising from precept and example, by which the observance of the rite is enforced, to its general threefold relation to the Father, the Son, and the Holy Spirit, to the reference it conveys to the effulgence and fullness of the gift of the Spirit in His overwhelming and all absorbing influence, as also to its significancy as a symbol of "the washing away of sins."

Its chief symbolical significancy as a Christian rite, appears in its relation to what is involved in a union with Christ in His death and resurrection. With the hope of contributing to a suitable appreciation of the nature of this relationship, and especially, of aiding in extending the important practical influence which is inseparable from a proper recognition of it, are the following suggestions introduced.

This significancy of the rite answers directly to the simple *import of its name;* and, in its relation to the work of Christ, it is repeatedly recognized in His own personal instructions, in those familiar allusions to baptism occuring in Luke 12: 50, and Mark 10: 38.

His baptism or submersion in death, it is worthy of notice, conveys no allusion to *cleansing,* as relating to Him as "baptized;" and yet it was, as it respects the figurative application of the term, distinctively and completely a "baptism." The reference is, not, it is true, to all the purposes pertaining to the rite in the whole range of its significancy, but to that which constitutes it specifically and properly "baptism." As such our Lord would have His disciples contemplate it in their use of the familiar forms of expression by which it is designated. As such it is specially significant, as associated with the most affecting and precious facts and truths of the gospel.

Whelming or submersion beneath extraordinary calamities or afflictions, or by the pressure of accumulated and overpowering evils of various kinds, as representing the meaning of the word "baptize," appertains to a common and well known usage of the ancient Greek language. No more naturally and certainly does the familiar expression, "overwhelming sufferings," fix the attention to the characteristic import of the word "overwhelm," than was the word "baptize," when applied to what were in reality excessive or overwhelming sufferings, adapted to bring irresistably before the mind the same generic idea. This usage finds a complete correspondence in the figurative representation of numerous passages in the Old Testament Scriptures, including the significant declaration in one of the Messianic Psalms, Ps. 69 : 2, where the Greek version of Symmachus has employed the identical term, "baptize," in the translation.

In this baptism of *suffering*, as distinguished from a ritual baptism, our Lord assured His disciples, as is expressed in Mark 10 : 39, that they would have occasion, as the floods of persecution should burst upon them, to "follow" Him as "sufferers with Him." But in some important respects, the baptism of the Master, in its nature and incidents, as also in its design, was, like the "cup" which might not pass from Him, peculiar. His death itself in its connection with the manifestation of the divine displeasure against sin, which attended it, was the great suffering which overwhelmed and submerged Him in its depths of darkness and of mystery. It was not a natural event. It came upon Him and passed over Him by no law of His intrinsic nature. His innocence and holiness, as also the principle of life which inhered in His divinity, naturally resisted it and rose above it.

There is, indeed, an original adaptation for this application of the figure, in its more general use. This is obvious from representations such as appear in Ps. 88 : 4—7, 16, 17, where the prophet compares his condition to that of one "afflicted with all the waves" of Jehovah's "fierce wrath," as it had "gone over" him, and who had been "laid in the lowest pit, in darkness, in the deeps," as "free among the dead," and "like the slain that lie in the grave." The description will suffice, at least, to show how naturally the conception of a baptism in suffering, when reaching its lowest depths, was associated, in the minds of the sacred writers, with the realities of death and the grave. A similar association of thought appears in Ps. 69 : 14, 15, and in Jon. 2 : 2—6. But, for Him who, even in anticipation of the event, in the overwhelming agony of His spirit, uttered the language recorded in Mat. 26 : 38, 39, death possessed an inner and mysterious depth of suffering and humiliation and darkness, which admits of no adequate description. What was involved in the vicarious submersion of Him who was life, in the elements of death, of Him who was "the Lord our righteousness," in the strange elements which *sin*, and the appointed work of atoning for it, had created, it is impossible for us to know.

Of such a baptism or submersion it may seem hardly necessary to remark, that it was endured for purposes of the highest *religious significancy*. Like the transaction in the rite, moreover, it involved the element of a definite and appointed accomplishment. A completion, an emerging, a resurrection is inseparable from the very conception of it as connected with the purposes for which it was required. "A baptism to be baptized with," is the form of our Savior's declaration. And, as an unmistakable indication that His descent into death must be identified with any proper apprehension of the events in which it was realized, the passage records the significant exclamation, " how am I straitened, till it be accomplished!" language which obviously refers directly to a release and an enlargement which were to be reached only by His resurrection from the dead. Comp. John 12 : 24.

Thus the idea of " baptism" is seen to be, even in the instructions of Christ himself, inseparably associated with His death and resurrection ; and this with direct and specific reference to the characteristic meaning of the term as denoting submersion. And surely we cannot fail to find the *symbol* in the import of a name which may thus be directly descriptive of the *reality*.

In beautiful harmony with this exposition of the import of baptism are the teachings of Christ respecting the distinctive relations and experience of the subjects of the rite. Notice John 3 : 16; Mat. 7 : 14 ; 8 : 22; John 5 : 24 ; 6 : 40; Luke 14 : 14 ; John 11 : 25 ; 5 : 21, 25—29 ; also Mat. 10 : 39 ; 16 : 25 ; Mark 8 : 35 ; Luke 9 : 24. Of the same nature also is the representation which accompanies that remarkable prediction of *His death and resurrection* which is recorded in John 12 : 23—28, and in which there is a distinct recognition of the essential union existing between Him and His "followers." With views and feelings answering to the import and spirit of the teachings thus indicated, He would have those who would " follow" Him, approach the baptismal waters, fully conscious that in passing beneath them, they were to take upon themselves a corresponding profession.

That which strikes the senses as most obvious in the act of Christian baptism, is the descent into the water, the burial, and the rising again. This is the aspect of the rite which its very name, in its simple import, brings before the mind, and with which, moreover, our Lord has taught us, in repeated allusions to this import of the name, to identify the very *idea* of "baptism." In this, its distinctively " baptismal" aspect, it has, both as a memorial rite, and an act of profession, a natural significance with reference to the facts which are directly *declarative* of the death and resurrection life of Christ,—a significance which extends equally to a declaration of the fellowship of His people with Him in both.

In the series of events pertaining to the work of redemption through the mediation of Christ, His BURIAL is assigned, in the representation of the Scriptures, a position of importance, as prominent as it is apparently significant and suggestive. This will be obvious by a simple reference to such passages as 1 Cor. 15: 4; Isa. 53: 9; Mat. 12: 39, 40; Acts 13: 29; Eph. 4: 8. A sufficient ground for this representation exists in the fact that His burial was the crowning *act* and *proof* of His vicarious humiliation unto death.

It is for a similar reason that a " burial" becomes appropriately and specially significant of the believer's *fellowship with Christ* in His death. It is a declaration of a death, not in process of accomplishment, but as actually *accomplished*. It indicates that " the world" and " sin," as also all hope of justification by "the law," are finally and fully renounced, in a participation of the soul in the blessings of Christ's finished work of humiliation and sacrifice.

Equally significant and instructive, in connection with the objects and exercise of Christian faith, is the position occupied by His RESURRECTION. It is the "appointed" and decisive proof, not only of His triumph over death and the powers of darkness, but of His entrance on a *new* and *glorious* life, in which, as an atoning Savior, He reigns as "Head over all things to the church." It is, in fact, through the medium of His resurrection that the sacred writers continually invite us to contemplate the reality of His life of mediation in His state of " exaltation" and "glory." And in any attempt to *represent* this reality and the blessings involved in it, to the senses, the symbol of a *resurrection* appears as being, not merely the most expressive, but the only natural and suitable transaction.

The coming forth from the emblematic grave, which is involved in the act of baptism, represents, not, as in the case of the burial, an event or experience accomplished, but a life which, while it is attained and enjoyed indeed, is only *entered upon*. It indicates a *transition* by which the subject has been brought into connection with Christ's glorious resurrection life; a blessedness which is to be consummated at the resurrection of the body, when, in his entire nature, he shall become conformed to the image of Him who is " the First-born among many brethren."

The design of Christ in His death and resurrection, was, not merely to " save sinners," in a general sense, but to make them, in their salvation, *one with Himself*. And in the baptism of His redeemed ones as His witnesses, His representatives, His " brethren," His " members," His death and resurrection are proclaimed to the world as the distinctive features of His gospel. In being " buried in baptism," they are buried "with *Him*." They are "baptized into *His* death." They signify that they "are risen with *Him*." The "death to sin" which is declared, is an actual *fellowship*, in purpose, in spirit, in experience, with Him in His death for the removal and destruction of sin. The resurrection which they profess to have experienced, is not merely an entrance upon a new and spiritual life, but a real participation in the blessedness of His own resurrection life.

It is thus seen that a union or fellowship with Christ in His death and resurrection, covers the *whole range* of Christian experience and character and blessing and hope. In professing this, in the rite appointed for the purpose, the believer makes, as he could appropriately do in no other way, a *complete profession* of whatever pertains to his religious privileges and duty and prospects, whether in relation to this life or that which is to come. His profession, moreover, is properly and pre-eminently a *characteristic* one. It is one in which are directly recognized and proclaimed his distinctive character and relations as a Christian. The act is expressive, not merely of consecration, of cleansing, of hope of forgiveness,—ideas which, in their generic application, are found also in association with most human systems of religion,—but of that by which the disciple of Christ as such is specially characterized and distinguished, in which the peculiar excellence and power and glory of his religion, both as a system of truth and as a soul-transforming influence, shine forth with distinct and characteristic light. The beautiful fitness of things which appears in this provision of the gospel, strikingly illustrates alike the wisdom of its Author, and its peculiar adaptation to answer the great purpose of its revelation.

The more fully we can identify CHRIST with the act of Christian profession, the more completely is the original design of such a profession attained.

In the observance of the Lord's Supper by Protestant churches, much is gained by a familiar and habitual reference to His own personal connection with its original institution. While we do not regard it as appointed for His especial benefit, with what interest and profit, nevertheless, do we contemplate Him as participating in the transaction, this first "breaking of bread," and as saying, "This is my body, which is broken for you,"—"This is my blood of the new testament, which is shed for you, for the remission of sins." But how seldom, in the observance of any act called "baptism," except where the original rite is retained, do we hear any such familiar allusion made to the *baptism* of our blessed Lord in the river Jordan. All those delightful associations of thought and feeling which such a reference is adapted to awaken in the mind, and all those incentives to obedience and devotion which naturally spring from a consideration of Christ's *example*, accordingly fail, in such a case, to reach the consciousness of the subject.

Similar in its tendency, although far more disastrous in the extent of the evil, is the prevalent disseverance from the act of Christian profession, of all significant or symbolical reference to the death, burial and resurrection of Jesus. Even in cases where there is not an actual omission of *all voluntary* subjection to a ritual observance, there is a failure to recognize and exhibit, as having any significant relation to the transaction, those interesting views of Christian doctrine and experience and character which are so prominently presented to view in Rom. 6 : 2—5, and Col. 2 : 12, 20; 3 : 1, 3. The subject of baptism, of the rite referred to in these passages, as having been observed by the primitive Christians, is naturally reminded, that, as he is "buried with Christ in baptism," so he is to regard himself as dead to sin and the world, one with Christ in the likeness and fellowship of His death; and that, "like as Christ was raised from the dead by the glory of the Father," so he is taking upon himself the symbol of His resurrection, and is henceforth to be visibly as well as really identified with His resurrection life; that this is what the ordinance *means*, what it was designed to show forth, and continually to recall to mind as involved in the very nature and import of his profession. But in the attempted substitution, in addition to the actual want of any such symbolical import in the act itself, the manifest *incongruity* which would be involved in an effort to associate with it this significancy, operates irresistibly to keep the characteristic nature of the Christian profession, as expressed in such an exposition, mostly or entirely out of sight.

Never will the witness of Christ's disciples be complete, or His gospel accomplish its full mission as a transforming influence in the world, until the power of His death and resurrection, and the duty and privilege of His people to be fully united or identified with these in their design and glorious results, are proclaimed, not merely from the pulpit, or on the printed page, but in the very *act of professing* His gospel. Nor, in another view, is there any other method or process by which the great body of believers will ever acquire for themselves, as a matter of personal consciousness, a full and adequate conception and appreciation of the distinctive nature and design of the Christian profession, or of the peculiarity and sacredness of the obligations which it involves. They must be able to read the claims resting upon them arising from their relation to their Savior's death and resurrection, in the very import of their profession. Their obligation to be identified with Him in these great facts of the work of redemption, must enter into every apprehension, every recognition, every recollection of that profession. This view of their relations and privileges and responsibility, must be incorporated with the very conception which they form of the nature and object of their separation from the world.

Neither reason nor faith can adequately estimate the preciousness and importance of the truth of Christ's resurrection life, as it is viewed in its three-fold relationship, first, to His own divine and infinite nature, secondly, to the nature which He possesses in common with His people, and, thirdly, to His work of mediation. By virtue of the incarnation, it exists in personal union with all the perfection of the Eternal Word. Existing no less truly in connection with a perfect humanity, it perpetually unites Him to "those who come unto God by Him," as their Elder Brother and sympathizing High Priest. And as being specifically a *resurrection* life, a life succeeding to His sacrificial humiliation unto death, it necessarily brings with it, and will ever possess all the efficacy of His work of atonement. The infinite merit of His vicarious sacrifice is continued as embodied and represented in His life. And in this, in its two-fold relation to "God" and "men," alone exists a "power" that is adequate to the work of redemption. In its intercessory relation to the government of God, it perpetually secures to those who are brought into union with it, all the blessings of a perfect righteousness and propitiation. In its relation to the agency by which the hearts of men are to be subdued and sanctified, it is inseparable from the purchased gift of the Holy Spirit, and furnishes occasion for the highest possible exercise of the moral influence of holy love and faith and devotion.

Such are the relations and nature and influence of the LIFE OF CHRIST as it is connected with the significancy of the rite of Christian profession. And it should be the joy of every thankful disciple, to seek to identify that significancy with his public life and character, and thus to acquire a position where He may, not only experience for himself the intended benefits of a *recognized* relationship to Christ, as one who "is risen with Him," but may also meet his solemn responsibility as one who, through this significancy of the rite, voluntarily assumed and transferred to himself, is to stand as a living and perpetual "witness" to the inestimable value of this distinguishing, all comprehensive, all pervading truth of the Christian revelation.

The preceding remarks will sufficiently indicate the grand design of this little volume. It has been the aim of the author to set forth in a form adapted, if possible, to arrest the attention, and to leave an impression on the memory and the heart, THE GREAT FACTS AND TRUTHS OF EVANGELICAL CHRISTIANITY. There never was a time when the hearts of Christians, to say nothing of others, needed to be drawn into closer *sympathy with Christ* in His work of humiliation and death for the destruction of sin, or to have brought more fully and vividly to their practical apprehension the doctrine of His resurrection life, and the various obligations and privileges and hopes which are intimately related to these cardinal points of doctrinal and experimental Christianity. And surely it ought not, with any Christian heart, to preclude, but rather deepen the interest which would otherwise be felt in the exhibition of these facts and truths, that they are presented in their proper relation to the rite of CHRISTIAN PROFESSION, a profession which, in the case of the primitive Christians, was indicative of the nature of their faith, and was regarded as *resting upon them in its significancy*, its obligations and its influence, through life. In what relation can they possibly be so appropriately presented? Where may we hope to see them exhibited in their most impressive and interesting light, if not in connection with a profession whose very design is to set forth the most clearly and significantly the nature of the truth and experience which are professed? *Doctrinal Christianity*, as being the doctrine especially of the execution and consummation of an infinite scheme of mercy, presents that consummation in the mediatorial *resurrection life* of the Son of God, resulting, with all its included blessings, from His divinely meritorious obedience and humiliation unto death. In this, as we have seen, His incarnation and sacrificial sufferings have their proper explanation and significancy; and in this their priceless value and saving power, including the transforming agency of the Holy Spirit, will ever be realized. *Experimental Christianity* is properly the *experience* of a new or *resurrection life*, involving a death to sin, and attained and enjoyed by virtue of a union with the life of Christ. And baptism, the initiatory rite of Christianity, the appointed badge of Christian character and relationship, is appropriately the profession, the formal declaration and avowal and significant representation of BOTH. Let it ever be identified with both, as it shall operate to bring them home in all their preciousness and controlling influence to the consciousness and heart of the Christian, and as the apprehension and recollection of them shall thus be associated with all that is most characteristic and most sacred and obligatory in his vows of public consecration and discipleship.

BAPTISMAL HYMNS.

THE THREEFOLD PROFESSION.

"Baptizing them IN THE NAME OF THE FATHER AND OF THE SON AND OF THE HOLY SPIRIT."—Mat. 28 : 19.

"Of whom, as concerning the flesh, Christ came, who is over all, God blessed forever."—Rom. 9 ; 5.

"He took part of the same, that through death He might destroy him that had the power of death."—Heb. 2 : 14.

"And He is the Head of the body, the church ; who is the beginning, the first born from the dead ; that in all things He might have the pre-eminence."—Col. 1 : 18.

"The SPIRIT OF HIM that raised up JESUS from the dead."—Rom. 8 : 11.

1 O'er our whole nature, God of grace,
   Assert Thy rightful sway ;
  Oh ! bathe us in the fount of life,
   And wash our sins away.

2 Jesus ! united to Thy death,
   Thy saving power we own ;
  Thou art our resurrection life ;
   We live by Thee alone.

3 Spirit of God ! we seek Thy grace,
   So rich, so full, so free ;
  Our souls, baptized in light and love,
   Would henceforth dwell in Thee.

4 To Thee, our God,—the Father, Son,
   And Comforter Divine,—
  To Thee, our hearts, our lives, our all,
   We thankfully resign.

See page 70.

BUNYAN.

CON DOLCEZZA. C. M. C. HATCH SMITH

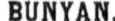

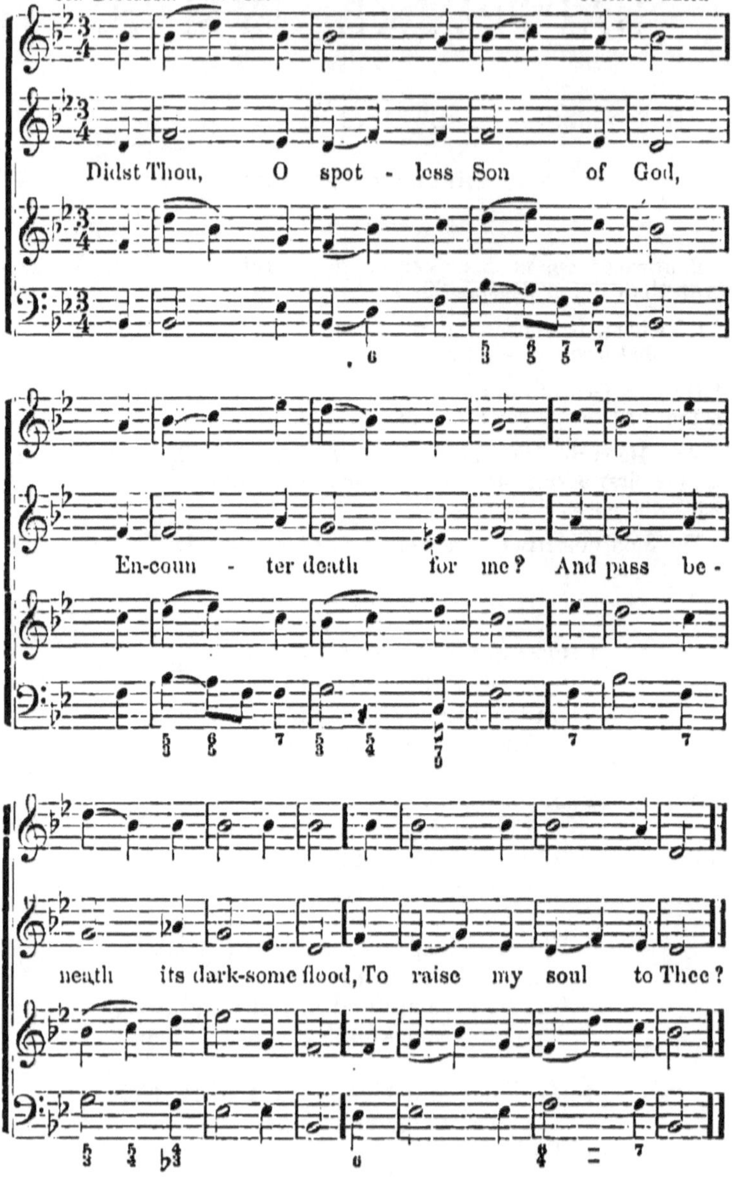

"THE LOVE OF CHRIST CONSTRAINETH US."

"The faith of the Son of God, who loved me, and gave himself for me."—Gal. 2 : 20.

"God commendeth His love toward us, in that, while we were yet sinners, Christ DIED FOR US."—Rom. 5 : 8.

"Know ye not that so many of us as were baptized into Jesus Christ, were BAPTIZED INTO HIS DEATH?"—Rom. 6 : 3.

"It is Christ that died, yea, rather, that is RISEN AGAIN, who is even at the right hand of God, who also maketh intercession for us."—Rom. 8 : 34, 35.

"Buried with Him in baptism, wherein also ye are risen WITH HIM, through the faith of the operation of God, who raised Him from the dead."—Col. 2 : 12.

"When they believed Philip preaching the things concerning the kingdom of God, and the name of Jesus Christ, they were baptized, both men and women."—"They were baptized in the name of the Lord Jesus."—Acts 8 : 12, 16.

---

1 Didst Thou, O spotless Son of God,
    Encounter death for me ?
And pass beneath its darksome flood,
    To raise my soul to Thee ?—

2 And shall I, while with joyous faith
    I trust Thy power to save,
Shrink from the emblem of that death,
    Thy love in wisdom gave ?

3 Didst Thou, to make Thy glory mine,
    Rise Conqueror from the strife ?—
And shall I spurn the blessed sign
    Which still proclaims Thy life ?

4 Oh ! shall I fear, for Thy dear name
    To sink beneath the wave ?
Be dead each thought of fear or shame,
    And buried in THY grave.

"WHAT MEAN YE BY THIS SERVICE."

"Jesus answered them, saying, The hour is come that the Son of man should be glorified. Verily, verily, I say unto you, Except a corn of wheat fall into the ground and die, it abideth alone ; but if it die, it bringeth forth much fruit. He that loveth his life shall lose it."— "If any man serve me, let him follow me."—John 12 : 23, 24, 25, 26.

"I lay down my life, that I might take it again."—"Because I live, ye shall live also."—John 10 : 17 ; 14 : 19.

"By the resurrection of Jesus Christ ; who is gone into heaven, and is on the right hand of God."—1 Pet. 3 : 21, 22. Comp. vs. 18—21.

"If we be dead with Christ, we believe that we shall also live with Him ; knowing that Christ being raised from the dead, dieth no more." —Rom. 6 : 8, 9. Compare verse 4.

"Knowing that He who raised up the Lord Jesus, shall raise up us also by Jesus, and shall present us with you."—1 Cor. 4 : 14.

"Christ the first fruits ; afterward they that are Christ's at His coming."—1 Cor. 15 : 23. Compare verse 29. See Note on page 96.

---

1 Oh ! there's a voice in this blest rite
 Which, far beyond the power of speech,
Can thrill the soul with pure delight,
 Where human accents fail to reach !

2 It speaks of Him who through the tomb
 Passed to His throne of light above,–
To faith dispelling all its gloom
 By the sweet radiance of His love.

3 With Him we die to earth and sin,
 Whose death alone has power to save ;—
With Him we rise to life divine,
 To wait our triumph o'er the grave.

4 Come, Gracious Spirit, from above ;
 Life, light and joy to us impart;
Speak, with Thy still, small voice of love,
 In silence to the inmost heart.

"IN THE NAME OF THE LORD JESUS."

"Buried with Him by baptism into death; that, like as Christ was raised up from the dead by the glory of the Father, even so we also should walk in newness of life."—Rom. 6: 4.

" Our Lord Jesus Christ, who died for us, that, whether we wake or sleep, we should live together with Him."—1 Thess. 5: 9, 10.

" He hath quickened us together with Christ, (by grace ye are saved,) and hath raised us up together, and made us sit together in heavenly places in Christ Jesus."—"Quickened together with Him."—Eph. 2: 5, 6; Col. 2: 13. Compare verse 12.

" According to the promise of life which is in Christ Jesus."—" Who hath abolished death, and hath brought life and immortality to light through the gospel."—2 Tim. 1: 2, 10. Compare chap. 2: 11.

" For your fellowship in the gospel from the first day until now."—" Among whom ye shine as lights in the world, holding forth the word of life."—Phil. 1: 5; 2: 15, 16. Compare Acts 16: 30—34, 40.

---

1 I will walk, in the joy of my Lord,
   In the light which His love has revealed.
Oh! why should the truth of His word,
   Or the power of His grace be concealed?

2 Oh! why should I shrink to confess
   My union with Him in His death,
Or my love for His name to express,
   In this beautiful emblem of faith?

3 Oh! why should I seek to disown
   The rite, by His wisdom ordained,
Where so clearly in symbol is shown
   The life which in Him is attained?

4 How brightly His mercy still gleams
   Through this precious memorial sign!
Oh! sweet is the truth it proclaims,
   That in DEATH and in LIFE He is mine!

"WHO DIED FOR THEM AND ROSE AGAIN"

"How shall we that are dead to sin, live any longer therein? Know ye not that so many of us as were baptized into Jesus Christ, were baptized into His death?"—Rom. 6: 2, 3.

"Dead with Christ from the rudiments of the world."—"Dead indeed unto sin, but alive unto God through Jesus Christ our Lord."—Col. 2: 20; Rom. 6: 11. Compare Gal. 2: 19.

"If we be dead with Him, we shall also live with Him."—"The Son quickeneth whom He will."—2 Tim. 2: 11; John 5: 21.

"If we have been planted together in the likeness of His death, we shall be also in the likeness of His resurrection."—Rom. 6: 5.

"Married to another, even to Him who is raised from the dead, that we should bring forth fruit unto God."—Rom. 7: 4.

"That they who live should not henceforth live unto themselves, but unto Him who died for them and rose again."—2 Cor. 5: 15.

"I esteem all Thy precepts concerning all things to be right."—"I will delight myself in Thy statutes."—Ps. 119: 128, 16.

---

1 Oh! sweet the sacred sign
   Of mercy full and free,
Where dying love and quick'ning power
   In mingled rays I see!

2 Oh! rich the wondrous grace
   Which brought salvation nigh,
Through Him who entered death's domain,
   And rose no more to die!

3 With Him I die to sin,
   The world and self disown;
And, raised to share His glorious life,
   I live to Him alone.

4 Jesus, my risen Lord,
   I love this sacred sign;
Planted with Thee in death, in life
   I shall be ever thine.

"THE ANSWER OF A GOOD CONSCIENCE TOWARD GOD."

"And they went down both into the water, both Philip and the eunuch; and he baptized him."—Acts 8: 38.

"And he received sight forthwith, and arose, and was baptized."—Acts 9: 18. Compare verse 6, and chap. 22: 10, 14—16.

"No man, when he hath lighted a candle, putteth it in a secret place, neither under a bushel, but on a candlestick, that they who come in may see the light."—Luke 11: 33. Compare Gal. 3: 27; Mat. 28: 19; Acts 2: 37, 38; 10: 47.

"If ye love me, keep my commandments."—John 14: 15.

"Who am I, and what is my people, that we should be able to offer so willingly after this sort?"—1 Chron. 29: 14.

---

1 How lovely the emblem of faith
   In Christ, our adorable Head,—
Who sought our redemption in death,
   And, triumphing, rose from the dead.

2 How sweet in this beautiful rite
   Our union with Him to proclaim,—
Our death to each sinful delight,—
   Our rising to life through His name.

3 How blessed, by bearing the cross,
   To show our regard for His will,—
To seek, while professing His cause,
   'All righteousness thus to fulfill.'

4 How pleasant the path to pursue
   His perfect example has led;
With th' scene at the Jordan in view,
   We haste in His footsteps to tread.

5 Dear Savior, Thine ordinance bless;
   The joy of Thy presence make known;
Descend, O Thou Spirit of grace,
   And seal us forever thine own.

See page 87.

DAY SPRING.

"HE REJOICED, BELIEVING IN GOD."

"Go ye into all the world, and preach the gospel to every creature. He that believeth and is baptized, shall be saved; but he that believeth not shall be damned."—Mark 16: 15, 16.

"And Crispus, the chief ruler of the synagogue, believed on the Lord, with all his house; and many of the Corinthians, hearing, believed, and were baptized."—Acts 18: 8.

"That ye walk worthy of the vocation wherewith ye are called, with all lowliness and meekness."—Eph. 4: 1, 2, 5.

"Speaking to yourselves in psalms and hymns and spiritual songs, singing and making melody in your heart to the Lord; giving thanks always for all things unto God and the Father, in the name of our Lord Jesus Christ."—Eph. 5: 19, 20.

"Rejoicing in hope, patient in tribulation."—"Looking for the mercy of our Lord Jesus Christ unto eternal life."—Rom. 12: 12; Jude 21.

"Set your affection on things above, not on things on the earth."—Col. 3: 2. Compare verse 1, and chap. 2: 12.

"The path of the just is as the shining light, that shineth more and more unto the perfect day."—Prov. 4: 19.

---

1 Meekly from the mystic flood
  Rising in thy Savior's name,
Meekly tread the heavenly road,
  And thy joy in Him proclaim.

2 Sweetly, on thy tuneful lyre,
  Strike the notes of thankful praise;
Sweetly, with th' angelic choir,
  Sing the glory of His grace.

3 Thus pursue thine upward path,
  E'er rejoicing on thy way,
'Till the day-spring light of faith
  Lead thee on to perfect day.

GRANVILLE.

Put on the Lord. If thou hast known The inward peace of sins for-given, If o'er thy con-trite soul has shone The joy of faith, the light of heaven.—

"ONE LORD, ONE FAITH, ONE BAPTISM."

"When they heard this, they were baptized IN THE NAME OF THE LORD JESUS."—Acts 19: 5.

"And he was baptized, he and all his, straightway. And when he had brought them into his house, he set meat before them, and rejoiced, believing in God with all his house."—Acts 16: 32, 33, 34.

"He that believeth and is baptized."—"Through the faith of the operation of God."—"One Lord, one faith, one baptism."—"Baptism,— the answer of a good CONSCIENCE toward God."—Mark 16: 16; Col. 2: 12; Eph.4: 5; 1 Pet. 3: 21.

"Ye are all the children of God BY FAITH in Christ Jesus."—"Not of blood, nor of the will of the flesh, nor of the will of man, but of God." —Gal. 3: 26; John 1: 13. Compare verse 12.

"Think not to say within yourselves, We have Abraham to our father."—"Every one of us shall give account of himself to God."— Mat. 3: 9; Rom. 14: 15.

"As many of you as have been baptized into Christ, have PUT ON CHRIST."—Gal. 3: 27.
See Note on page 96.

---

1 Put on the Lord. If thou hast known
  The inward peace of sins forgiven,
 If o'er thy contrite soul has shone
  The joy of faith, the light of heaven,

2 Put on the Lord; O, haste to prove
  Thy severance from the bonds of earth;
 Haste, in the ardor of thy love,
  To own thy new and heavenly birth.

3 Haste to proclaim that thou by faith
  Art one with Christ, thy living Head,—
 One, in the likeness of His death,—
  One, in His rising from the dead.

4 'Tis for thyself, with conscious zeal,
  In this blest rite, to own thy Lord;
 'Tis for thyself to do His will,
  In glad obedience to His word.

"REPENT AND BE BAPTIZED EVERY ONE OF YOU."

"And he commanded them to be baptized in the name of the Lord." —Acts 10 : 48.

"When ye received the word of God, which ye heard of us, ye received it, not as the word of men, but, as it is in truth, the word of God, which effectually worketh also in you that believe."—1 Thess. 3 : 13.

"He therefore that despiseth, despiseth not man, but God, who hath also given unto us His Holy Spirit."—1 Thess. 4 : 8. Comp. ver. 1.

"Ye became followers of us, and of the Lord, having received the word in much affliction.—1 Thess. 1 : 6.

"They that gladly received his word, were baptized."—Acts 2 : 41.

"Repent, and be baptized, every one of you, in the name of Jesus Christ."—Acts 2 : 38.

---

1 Once more resounds the heavenly word,
   'Repent and be baptized.'—
And shall the voice of Christ, thy **Lord**,
   Be still despised ?

2 Oh ! shall a thankful, contrite heart
   His claim of love disown,
Whilst all thou hast and all thou art
   Are His alone ?

3 Shall the vain strife for worldly ease
   Thy ransomed powers employ ?
In glad obedience find thy peace,
   Thy light and joy.

4 Oh ! chide thy sloth, all fear repel,
   And haste to do His will ;
Nor let thy pride, with magic spell,
   Control thee still.

5 Rise in the strength of faith and **love**,
   And burst the tempter's chain ;
Nor doubt thy sacrifice shall prove
   Thy highest gain.

"WHY TARRIEST THOU? ARISE AND BE BAPTIZED."

"Christ also hath once suffered for sins, the just for the unjust, that He might bring us to God, being put to death in the flesh, but quickened by the Spirit."—1 Pet. 3: 18. Compare verse 21.

"Forasmuch then as Christ hath suffered FOR US in the flesh, arm yourselves likewise with the same mind."—1 Pet. 4: 1.

"The chastisement of our peace was upon Him."—"He made His GRAVE with the wicked, and with the rich in His death."—Isa. 53: 5, 9.

"They took Him down from the tree, and laid Him in a SEPULCHRE. But God raised Him from the dead."—Acts 13: 29, 30.

"BURIED WITH HIM IN BAPTISM, wherein also ye are risen with Him, through the faith of the operation of God, who raised Him from the dead."—Col. 2: 12.

---

1 Why linger on the brink
   Of Jordan's sacred flood?
Why, with the faith of Jesus, shrink
   To follow where He trod?

2 Oh! fear not pain or loss;
   Arise, and be baptized;
Thy Lord for thee endured the cross,
   For thee the shame despised.

3 For thee He sought the tomb
   To dwell among the dead;
For thee He rose, and o'er its gloom
   A peaceful radiance shed.

4 If one with Him in death,
   In life and glory one,
Here, in the joy of love and faith,
   The blissful union own.

•5 Here, buried in His name,
   Thy death to sin confess;
Thy resurrection life proclaim,
   Quicken'd and saved by grace.

HANSON PLACE.

"COME, SEE THE PLACE WHERE THE LORD LAY."

"Now in the place where He was crucified, there was a garden; and in the garden a new sepulchre, wherein was man never yet laid. There laid they Jesus."—John 19 : 41, 42.

"In the heart of the earth."—Mat. 12 : 40. "And after three days rise again."—Mark 8 : 31. "There shall no sign be given to it, but the sign of the prophet Jonas."—Mat 12 : 39.

"Thus it is written, and thus it behoved Christ to suffer, and to rise from the dead the third day."—Luke 24 : 46.

"The angel answered and said:"—"He is not here; for He is risen, as He said. Come, see the place where the Lord lay."—Mat. 28 : 5, 6.

"Buried WITH HIM by BAPTISM."—Rom. 6 : 4. "Know ye not that your bodies are the members of Christ?"—1 Cor. 6 : 15. Comp. v. 14.

"Now is Christ risen from the dead, and become the first fruits of them that slept."—1 Cor. 15 : 20. "Baptized into Christ, (ye) have PUT ON CHRIST."—"Risen with Him."—"Waiting for the adoption."—Gal. 3 : 27; 1 : 1; 2 : 20; Col. 2 : 12; Rom. 8 : 23.   See Note on page 97.

---

1 Not still on Calvary's brow,
  Within the garden wall,
We find the place where Jesus lay,
  Or hear the angel's call.

2 But here, in this blest rite,
  We see the Savior's tomb;
And hither, with adoring hearts,
  His people still may come.

3 As with exultant faith
  They view their risen Lord,
They here may on His mystic grave
  Their thankful vows record.

4 Fain would my throbbing heart
  The angel's call obey,
And haste in this loved sign to find
  The place where Jesus lay.

MAYVILLE.

L. M. T. E. PERKINS.

1 He broke the fell de-stroy-er's reign, And took the keys of hell and death; And o'er the val-ley of the slain, Now sheds His life- in-spir-ing breath.

"THE POWER OF HIS RESURRECTION."

"Christ is the end of the law for righteousness to every one that believeth."—"If we believe on Him that raised up Jesus our Lord from the dead; who was delivered for our offences, and was raised again for our justification. Therefore, being justified by faith, we have peace with God, through our Lord Jesus Christ,"—"and rejoice in hope of the glory of God."—Rom. 10 : 4 ; 4 : 24, 25 ; 5 : 1, 2.

"After He had offered one sacrifice for sins, forever sat down on the right hand of God ; from henceforth expecting till His enemies be made His footstool."—Heb: 10 : 12, 13.

"Always bearing about in the body the dying of the Lord Jesus, that the LIFE also of Jesus might be made manifest in our body."—"So then death worketh in us, but LIFE IN YOU."—2 Cor. 4 : 10, 12.

"You hath He quickened, who were dead in trespasses and sins,"—"fulfilling the desires of the flesh and of the mind."—"Quickened us together with Christ."—Eph. 2 : 1, 3, 5.

"He that believeth on me, though he were dead, yet shall he live."—John 11 : 25.

---

1 Oh! there's a power in Jesus' life
   To raise the soul from earth to heaven,
To heal the vain, perplexing strife
   Of hearts to pride and avarice given !

2 His righteousness the law fulfilled ;
   His sacrifice atoned for sin ;
And in His life, to faith revealed,
   Our life, our hope, our joy, begin.

3 He broke the fell destroyer's reign,
   And took the ' keys of hell and death,'
And o'er the valley of ' the slain'
   Now sheds His life-inspiring breath.

4 Oh ! sweet the monumental rite,
   Which stands, amidst earth's din and strife,
To point, with witness clear and bright,
   To JESUS' RESURRECTION LIFE !

"FOR A MEMORIAL FOR EVER."---Josh. 4: 7.

"And hath translated us into the kingdom of His dear Son."—"Who is the head of all principality and power."—"Who shall judge the quick and the dead at His appearing."—Col. 1: 13; 2: 10; 2 Tim. 4: 1.

"Whereof He hath given assurance unto all men, in that He hath raised Him from the dead."—"That I may know Him, and the power of His resurrection."—Acts 17: 31; Phil. 3: 10.

"With great power gave the apostles witness of the resurrection of the Lord Jesus."—Acts 4: 33; 2: 32.

"By above five hundred brethren at once, of whom the greater part remain unto this present; but some are fallen asleep."—"That ye may be able, after my decease, to have these things always in remembrance."—1 Cor. 15; 6; 2 Pet. 1: 15.

"This second EPISTLE, beloved, I now write unto you."—"The same commit thou to faithful MEN, who shall be able to teach others also."— 2 Pet. 3: 1; 2 Tim. 2: 2.

"As often as ye eat this BREAD, and drink this CUP, ye do show the Lord's death TILL HE COME."—1 Cor. 11: 26.

"One Lord, one faith, one BAPTISM."—"Wherein also ye are RISEN WITH HIM."—"Teach all nations, baptizing them,"—"and, lo, I am with you alway, even UNTO THE END OF THE WORLD."—Eph. 4: 5; Col. 2: 12; Mat. 28: 19, 20; Mark 16: 16, 19; Luke 24: 49, 50.   See Note on page 93

---

1 How precious this memorial sign,
   This pledge of life to come,
As sweetly bursts upon my sight
   The Savior's rending tomb!

2 In Jordan's hallowed stream He bowed,
   And blessed the sacred rite;
He rose from death's baptismal flood,
   To glorious life and light;—

3 Then stood on Olives' brow, and left
   The monumental sign.
Inscribing there my name, I own
   The grace and PROMISE mine.

"ALWAY, EVEN UNTO THE END OF THE WORLD."

" His name shall be continued as long as the sun; and men shall be blessed in Him."—" They shall fear Thee as long as the sun and moon endure, throughout all generations."—Ps. 72 : 17, 5.

" I am He that liveth, and was dead ; and, behold, I am alive for evermore, Amen; and have the keys of hell and of death. Write the things which thou hast seen, and the things which are, and the things which shall be HEREAFTER."—Rev. 1 : 18, 19.

" Having the everlasting gospel to preach unto them that dwell on the earth, and to every nation, and kindred, and tongue, and people.—Rev. 14: 6. Compare Dan. 7: 14; Ps. 22: 27.

" The like figure whereunto, even baptism, doth also now save us, not the putting away of the filth of the flesh, but the answer of a good conscience toward God, BY THE RESURRECTION OF JESUS CHRIST; who is gone into heaven, and IS ON THE RIGHT HAND OF GOD."—1 Pet. 3: 21, 22. Compare Ps. 110: 1, also Phil. 1 : 19; 2 Cor. 1 : 6.

" If ye be risen with Christ."—" When Christ, who is OUR LIFE, shall appear."—Col. 3: 1, 4. Compare chap. 2: 12, 13. See Note on page 93.

---

1. His kingdom shall ever increase,
   His name to all time be confessed ;
As long as the moon shall endure,
   In Him shall the nations be blessed.

2. As the Hope and Desire of His saints,
   His promise is ever the same ;
And, confessing our faith in His life,
   We still are baptized in His name.

3. Through all ages this sign shall remain ;
   In all lands shall its witness be known,
As it speaks of the life-giving power
   Of the Risen and Glorified One.

4. It shall show, that the church in her life
   Is one with her covenant Head,
Till, in glory arrayed, He shall come
   As the Judge of the quick and the dead.

STRATFIELD.—CONCLUDED.

"IN HOPE OF THE GLORY OF GOD."

" And when they were come up out of the water, the Spirit of the Lord caught away Philip, that the eunuch saw him no more; and he went on his way rejoicing."—Acts 8: 39.

" We rejoice in hope of the glory of God."—" We walk by faith, not by sight;"—" willing rather to be absent from the body, and to be present with the Lord."—" Of whom the whole family in heaven and earth is named."—Rom. 5: 2; 2 Cor. 5: 7, 8; Eph. 3: 15.

" Jesus said unto him, Verily, I say unto thee, To day shalt thou be with me in paradise."—" Fear not them that kill the body, but are not able to kill the soul."—Luke 23: 43; Mat. 10: 28.

" God hath both raised up the Lord, and will also raise up us by His own power. Know ye not that your bodies are the members of Christ?"—" Who shall change our vile body, that it may be fashioned like unto His glorious body."—1 Cor. 6: 14, 15; Phil. 3: 21.

" It is sown in corruption; it is raised in incorruption: it is sown in dishonor; it is raised in glory."—" As we have borne the image of the earthy, we shall also bear the image of the heavenly."—" Who is—the First-begotten of the dead."—1 Cor. 15: 42, 43, 49; Rev. 1: 5.

" If we believe that Jesus DIED and ROSE AGAIN, even so them also who sleep in Jesus, will God bring with Him."—1 Thess. 4: 14. Comp. Rom. 8: 17, 23; 1 Pet. 1: 3, 21; Phil. 3: 10—14; Cor. 15: 23.

" Else what shall they do who are baptized for the dead?"—1 Cor. 15: 29. See Note on page 99.

---

1 Our former hopes are slain,
   And buried from our sight;
   Raised to a new and heavenly life,
    We trace the path of light.

2 Up from the sacred flood,
   Rejoicing in our Head,
   We rise in witness of the power
    Which raised Him from the dead.

3 With lively hope we wait
   The resurrection day;
   We press to reach the promised prize
    Rejoicing on our way.

See page 86.

"THE GOSPEL WHICH YE HAVE RECEIVED."

"I declare unto you the gospel which I preached unto you, which also ye have received."—"For I delivered unto you, first of all, that which I also received, how that Christ DIED FOR OUR SINS according to the Scriptures; and that He was BURIED; and that He ROSE AGAIN the third day according to the Scriptures."—1 Cor. 15: 1, 3, 4. Compare verse 29, and Rom. 6: 3, 4.

"Now that He ascended, what is it but that He also descended first into the lower parts of the earth?"—Eph. 4: 9.

"The Son of man came not to be ministered unto, but to minister, and to give His life a ransom for many."—Mark 10: 45.

"His power to us-ward who believe, according to the working of His mighty power which He wrought in Christ, when He raised Him from the dead, and set Him at His own right hand in the heavenly places.—Eph. 1: 19, 20.

"Reconciled to God by the DEATH of His Son."—"Much more, being reconciled, we shall be saved by His LIFE."—Rom. 5: 10. [see page 15.]

---

1 Jesus, we love this sacred rite,
   In which Thy perfect work is shown,—
In which is seen, so clear, so bright,
   The grace we gladly seek to own.

2 To show Thy sin-atoning death
   We sink beneath the yielding wave,—
And rising—to the eye of faith
   Appears Thy triumph o'er the grave.

3 Thy death—Thy life—to these we owe
   The gracious change we now profess;
These are the source whence richly flow
   The varied blessings of Thy grace.

4 How sweet, while thus we own the Name
   We trust to save our souls from guilt,
In this blest emblem to proclaim
   The ground on which our hope is built!

HAMILTON.

"AND HE WAS BAPTIZED OF JOHN IN JORDAN."

"And He was baptized of John in Jordan. And straightway coming up out of the water, He saw the heavens opened, and the Spirit like a dove descending upon Him. And there came a voice from heaven, saying, Thou art my beloved Son, in whom I am well pleased."—Mark 1 : 9—11.

"Thus it becometh us."—Mat. 3 : 15.

"I delight to do Thy will, O my God; yea, Thy law is within my heart."—Ps. 40 : 8.

"And He will teach us of His ways; and we will walk in His paths."—Isa. 2 : 3.

---

1 Beside this placid pool
   We wait Thy blessing, Lord;
Here in Thy name we meet,
   Obedient to Thy word;
Thy gracious promise now fulfill,
And in the midst Thyself reveal.

2 As on Thy sacred head,
   In Jordan's hallowed stream,
Descending from on high,
   The Holy Spirit came,
In emblem of the peaceful dove,
To seal Thy mission from above,—

3 So now, as in this rite,
   We in Thy footsteps tread,
On us His precious gifts
   In rich profusion shed;
His peaceful influence now impart,
To sit and dwell on every heart.

4 With Thine approving smile
   This act of homage crown;
Our sacrifice accept,
   And seal us for thine own;
Thine we would be to serve Thee here,
And thine in glory to appear.

STENNETT.

"WHAT DOTH HINDER ME TO BE BAPTIZED."

"And he began at the same Scripture, and preached unto him JESUS. And as they went on their way, they came unto a certain water; and the eunuch said, See, here is water; what doth hinder me to be baptized?—Acts 8 : 35, 36. Comp. Isa. 53 : 7—11.

1 Didst thou tell me of the Savior?—
   Of the Just and Guileless One?—
How His soul was made an offering
   For the crimes which we had done?—

2 How He passed from crucifixion
   To the darkness of the grave?—
How, as risen, He lives in glory,
   Evermore to bless and save?—

3 How, in emblem of His passion,
   Once He bowed in Jordan's stream?—
How His love the same blest symbol
   Left for those who trust His name?—

4 Here is water; what doth hinder
   ME with Him to be baptized?
Fain I would be owned His follower,
   Howsoe'er by man despised.

5 What doth hinder? shall I cherish
   Aught of fear or worldly pride,
While the sign itself reminds me,
   For my ransom Jesus DIED?

6 What doth hinder? Oh! could suffering,
   Loss of friends, reproach or shame
Quench the love my thankful spirit
   Bears for His most precious name?

7 Let me follow in His footsteps;—
   Should I seek to shun the cross?—
Let me for His blessed service
   Count each transient gain but loss.

"PURSUING HIS FOOTSTEPS."

"That ye should show forth the praises of Him who hath called you."—1 Pet. 2: 9. Compare 1 Thess. 1: 6—10.

"Whether we live, we live unto the Lord; and whether we die, we die unto the Lord."—Rom. 14: 8.

"For to this end Christ both died, and rose and revived, that He might be Lord both of the dead and living."—Rom. 14: 9.

"He is able to save them to the uttermost that come unto God by Him, seeing He EVER LIVETH to make intercession for them."—Heb. 7: 25. Compare Rom. 8: 34.

"Then shall be brought to pass the saying that is written, Death is swallowed up in the victory. O death, where is thy sting? O grave, where is thy victory?"—"Thanks be to God, who giveth us the victory THROUGH OUR LORD JESUS CHRIST."—1 Cor. 15: 54, 55, 57. Compare verse 29.

---

1. In the joy of the Spirit,
    I will follow my Lord;
  He hath shed o'er my pathway
    The light of His word;
  His wisdom assures me
    His statutes are right;
  His commands are not grievous;
    His burden is light.
        Pursuing His footsteps,
          I bow 'neath the wave;
        And rising, proclaim Him,
          The Mighty to save.

2. To procure my redemption
    He hath passed through the tomb
  And the light of His glory
    Hath shed o'er its gloom.—
  I haste, with rejoicing,
    His grace to proclaim;
  And will 'show forth His praises,'
    While owning His name. .
        Pursuing, &c.

"AS THOSE THAT ARE ALIVE FROM THE DEAD."

"If ye then be risen with Christ, seek those things which are above, where Christ sitteth on the right hand of God."—Col. 3 : 1.

"Looking unto Jesus, the author and finisher of our faith."—"Who is our hope."—Heb. 12 : 2 ; 1 Tim. 1 : 1. Compare 2 Cor. 5 : 6—8.

"These things saith the First and the Last, who was dead, and is alive:"—"Be thou faithful unto death, and I will give thee a crown of life."—Rev. 2 : 8, 10. Compare Phil. 3 : 10—14.

"In whom, though now ye see Him not, yet believing ye rejoice with joy unspeakable and full of glory."—1 Pet. 1: 8.

---

1 Risen with Christ,—to things above
   In our faith aspiring,—
In the ardor of our hope
   Him alone desiring,—
We will walk as 'pilgrims here,'
Till in glory we appear ;—
    Singing, on our way to heaven,
      Glory, glory, glory !

2 With Him in His dying love
   Still in sweet communion,
To His resurrection life
   Joined in closest union,
We will spurn the world's control,
While we press to reach the goal ;
    Singing, on our way to heaven,
      Glory, glory, glory!

3 Faith that glory shall reveal
   To our raptured vision,
Till shall burst upon our view
   Glory in fruition,—
Till, released from toil and strife,
We shall take the crown of life ,—
    Singing, in the courts of heaven,
      Glory, glory, glory !

See tune on pages 89 and 99, also on next page.

"WELCOME TO OUR HAPPY BAND."

" Who have obtained like precious faith with us."—"Called unto the fellowship of His Son, Jesus Christ our Lord."—" Strangers and pilgrims."—2 Pet. 1: 1; 1 Cor. 1: 9; 1 Pet. 2: 11. Comp. Heb. 13: 14.

" For the hope which is laid up for you in heaven."—" Christ in you, the hope of glory."—" Christ who is our life."—" Christ is all, and in all."—" Buried with Him in baptism."—Col. 1: 5, 27; 3: 4, 11; 2: 12. Compare Gal. 3: 26—29; Eph. 4: 1—5; 1: 18. See Note on page 100.

---

1 Welcome,—from the whelming wave
 With your Savior rising,—
Joyous in His power to save,—
 Earthly hopes despising,—
Welcome to our happy band,
Pilgrims to a brighter land,
With us pressing on to glory.
 Glory, glory, glory !
We shall reign with Christ in glory.

2 Dead with Him who died for you,
 Dead to sin and folly,
Risen with Him to live anew,
 Live to trust Him wholly ;
Let each worldly striving cease ;
He is all your life and peace,—
' Christ in you the hope of glory.'
 Glory, glory, glory !
We shall reign with Him in glory.

3 Then will we, in worlds above,
 Join the rapturous chorus,
With the sea of light and love
 Ever bursting o'er us.
Christ who died, shall be our song ;
Christ our Life, each note prolong.
" Glory be to God for ever !
 " Glory, glory, glory !
" To the Lamb be endless glory !"

TAYLOR.

C.M. C. Hatch Smith.

Like some o'er-whelm-ing, rush-ing wind, Come in Thy love and might; Come like the sun's ef-ful-gent rays, And bathe our souls in light.

"THE SPIRIT OF GLORY."

"When there came such a voice to Him from the excellent glory."—"A bright cloud overshadowed them, and, behold, a voice out of the cloud."—"And they feared as they ENTERED INTO THE CLOUD."—2 Pet. 1:17; Mat. 17:5; Luke 9:34 Compare Luke 2:9.

"The glory of the Lord appeared in the cloud."—"And the glory of the Lord abode on mount Sinai; and the cloud covered it six days, and the seventh day He called unto Moses out of the midst of the cloud."—"And Moses went into the midst of the cloud."—Ex. 16:10; 24:16, 18.

"And he was there with the Lord forty days and forty nights."—"And when Aaron and all the children of Israel saw Moses, behold, the skin of his face shone."—Ex. 34:28, 30.

"How shall not the ministration of the Spirit be rather glorious?"—"God having provided some better thing for us."—2 Cor 3:8; Heb. 11:40. Compare Heb. 10:29; 2 Cor. 3:17, 18; John 7:39.

"For upon all the glory shall be a defence" (or covering—see marginal reading.)—Isa. 4:5. Compare Num. 16:42.

"The Spirit of glory and of God RESTETH UPON YOU."—1 Pet. 4:14.

"Which He shed on us ABUNDANTLY, through Jesus Christ our Savior."—Tit. 3:6.   See Note on page 100.

---

1 Spirit of glory and of God,
    Descend and fill the place;
  Come, Gift Divine, and o'er us shed
    The fullness of Thy grace.

2 Like some o'erwhelming, rushing wind,
    Come in Thy love and might;
  Come like the sun's effulgent rays,
    And bathe our souls in light.

3 As here, repentant for our sin,
    We bow beneath the flood,
  So into Thee we sink from self
    To dwell with Christ in God.

HERBERTSVILLE.

BAPTISMAL HYMNS. 57

The two following hymns, with the exception of the last stanza in each, were written without reference to any special relation of them to baptism. They are taken from a manuscript volume of a more general character, now in readiness for publication, and are here inserted, with the addition indicated, on account of their adaption to express the feelings naturally cherished in connection with a proper observance of this ordinance.

"FOR TO ME TO LIVE IS CHRIST."

" Who of God is made unto us wisdom, and righteousness, and sanctification, and redemption."—" I live, yet not I, but Christ liveth in me."—1 Cor. 1: 30; Gal. 2: 20.

" Other foundation can no man lay than that is laid, which is Jesus Christ."—" Ye are Christ's."—" By whom are all things, and we by Him."—" Was Paul crucified for you? or were ye BAPTIZED in the name of Paul?"—1 Cor. 3: 11, 23; 8: 6; 1: 13.

1 Jesus, by Thy precious merit,
   Free me from the guilt of sin;
By Thine all-creative Spirit,
   Form my nature pure within.

2 Make me humble, make me holy;
   May my heart with love o'erflow;
Make me kind and meek and lowly,
   As Thou wast while here below.

3 Humbly on Thy holy altar
   Life, with all its hopes, I lay;
Leave, O, leave me not to falter;
   Help me still to watch and pray.

4 Following in the path of duty,
   Free from anxious care and strife,
May I serve Thee in the beauty
   Of a pure and heavenly life.

5 Let this emblem of Thy passion
   Still remind me of Thy love;
Risen in hope of full salvation,
   Let me seek the things above.

"BATHED IN THE FOUNTAIN OF THY LOVE."

"But ye are washed, but ye are sanctified, but ye are justified, in the name of the Lord Jesus, and by the Spirit of our God."—1 Cor. 6: 11. Compare Heb. 13: 13, 14; Rev. 21: 23.

"Ye are not your own; for ye are bought with a price: therefore, glorify God in your body, and in your spirit, which are God's."—"Forgetting those things which are behind, and reaching forth unto those things which are before."—1 Cor. 6: 19, 20; Phil. 3: 13.

1 My God, to Thy supreme control
   My all I would resign;
 Oh! come and sanctify my soul,
   And make me wholly thine.

2 Oh! is there aught in earth to lure
   My heart from Thee astray?
 Soon will its joys, at best impure,
   Forever pass away.

3 Oh! is there aught in self to claim
   The love Thou dost require?
 Oh! be Thy service all my aim,
   Thy will my sole desire.

4 Oh! is there aught in sin to tempt
   The soul that, once renewed,
 Seeks from its power to be exempt,
   And find its all in God?

5 O Jesus, set me wholly free
   From earth and self and sin;
 Thou only canst complete for me
   The work Thou didst begin.

6 Bathed in the fountain of Thy love
   For sin's pollution given,
 I wait to bathe my soul anew
   In the pure light of heaven.

"THY BILLOWS ARE GONE OVER ME."

"Ye shall indeed drink of the cup that I drink of; and with the baptism that I am baptized with shall ye be baptized."—Mark 10 : 39.

"He hath made Him to be sin for us, who knew no sin."—2 Cor. 5 : 21.

"Thou hast afflicted me with all Thy waves."—Ps. 88 : 7.

"All Thy waves and Thy billows are gone over me."—Ps. 42 : 7.

"When my spirit was overwhelmed within me, then Thou knewest my path."—142 : 3.

"But He for our profit, that we might be partakers of His holiness."—Heb. 12 : 10.

"As the sufferings of Christ abound in us, so our consolation also aboundeth by Christ."—2 Cor. 1 : 5.   See Note on page 100.

1 Ye know not what ye ask :—
   The path to glory lies
 Along the rough and thorny vale
   Of toil and sacrifice.

2 Your wayward hearts must learn
   How vain is all below,
 As oft upon your lips is pressed
   The cup of keenest woe.

3 Your souls must oft be plunged
   Beneath the swelling flood,
 Till from that dark baptismal stream
   Ye rise to live for God,—

4 To find in Him your all,
   To trust His grace alone,
 And, in each conscious act of life,
   To make His will your own.

5 Then peace and joy divine
   Shall keep your minds and hearts,
 Then shall ye know the hidden bliss
   The life of God imparts.

ACCEPTANCE.

THE TWOFOLD BAPTISM.

"Thus it becometh us to fulfill all righteousness."—Mat. 3:15.

"I have a baptism to be baptized with; and how am I straitened till it be accomplished!"—Luke, 12:50.

"I am come into deep waters, where the floods overflow me."—Ps. 69:2   Compare verses 4,9; John, 15:26; 2:17; Rom. 15:3; Ps. 42:7; 88:6,7,16.

"My soul is exceeding sorrowful, even UNTO DEATH."—Mat. 26:38.

See Note on page 161.

---

1 Thus must the glorious Prince of life
 All righteousness fulfill,
In emblem of that fearful strife,
 When, by the Father's will,
He sank beneath death's darker flood,
And angels saw Him bathed in blood.

2 Oft had the covenant king and sire,
 From depths of anguish, cried:
"I sink, O God, beneath Thine ire;
 "In fierce and wrathful tide,
"Thy waves and billows o'er me roll;
"Deep upon deep o'erwhelms my soul."

3 So must th' Anointed Son and Lord,
 Of David's chosen seed,
By hell assailed, by man abhorred,
 O'erwhelmed in darkness, plead:
"My God, my God, why hast Thou left
"Thy Son to die, of light bereft?"

4 Oh! may I view, with contrite soul,
 That dark baptismal scene,—
Till, dead to self and sin's control,
 With faith and hope serene
I rise with Him, to share the bliss
Of His ACCEPTED righteousness.

BAPTISMAL HYMNS. 67

THE TWOFOLD BAPTISM.—CONTINUED.

king and sire, From depths of an-guish, cried: "I sink, O God, beneath Thine ire; In fierce and wrathful tide, Thy waves and bil-lows o'er me roll; Deep up-on deep o'er-whelms my soul."

3 So must th'A-noint-ed Son and Lord, Of

BAPTISMAL HYMNS.

THE TWOFOLD BAPTISM.—CONCLUDED.

CINCINNATI.

C. M. See page 13. WM. B. BRADBURY.

1 O'er our whole nature, God of grace,
  Assert Thy rightful sway;
  Oh! bathe us in the fount of power we own;
  And wash our sins away.

2 Jesus! united to Thy death,
  Thy saving life;
  Thou art our resurrection life;
  We live by Thee alone.

3 Spirit of God! we seek thy grace,
  So rich, so full, so free!
  Our souls, baptized in light and love,
  Would henceforth dwell in Thee.

4 To Thee, our God,—the Father, Son,
  And Comforter Divine,—
  To Thee, our hearts, our lives, our all,
  We thankfully resign.

BAPTISMAL HYMNS.

DOXOLOGY.

M. COLBURN.

Baptized in Thy thrice precious name, Thy blessing, O God, we implore, The praise of the Father proclaim, The Son and the Spirit adore.

DOXOLOGY.

"Grace, mercy and peace from God the Father, and the Lord Jesus Christ our Savior."—Tit. 1 : 4.

"And the Word was made flesh, and dwelt among us."—John 1 : 1, 14. "God blessed forever."—Rom. 9 : 5.

"Grieve not the Holy Spirit of God."—Eph. 4 : 30. "Not—unto men, but unto God."—Acts 5 : 4. Compare verse 3.

1 Baptized in Thy thrice precious name,
　Thy blessing, O God, we implore,—
　The praise of the Father proclaim,
　The Son and the Spirit adore.

2 Thy love is the joy of our heart;
　We trust in Thy wisdom and might;
　Our hope and salvation Thou art,
　Our portion, our life and our light.

EMBLEM.*

[CHANT.]

C. HATCH SMITH.

Moderato. QUARTETTE OR SEMI-CHORUS.

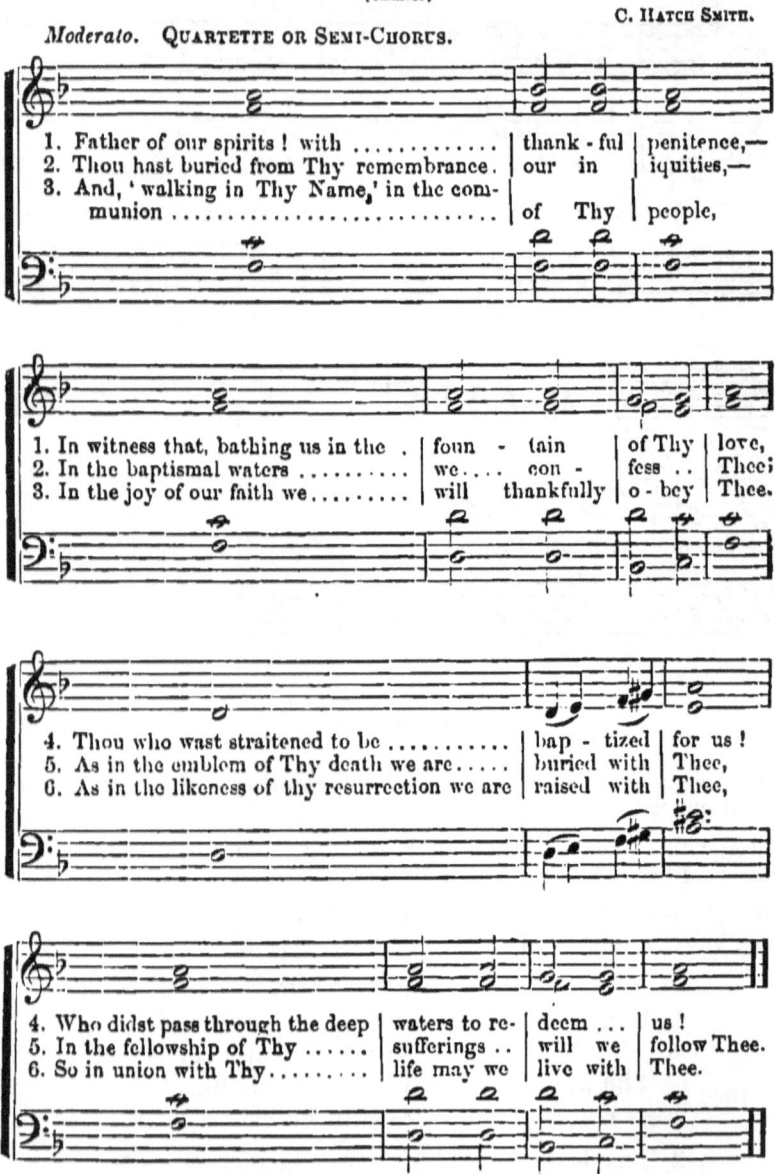

1. Father of our spirits! with .... | thank - ful | penitence,—
2. Thou hast buried from Thy remembrance. | our in | iquities,—
3. And, 'walking in Thy Name,' in the communion .... | of Thy | people,

1. In witness that, bathing us in the . | foun - tain | of Thy | love,
2. In the baptismal waters .... | we .... con - | fess .. | Thee;
3. In the joy of our faith we .... | will thankfully | o - bey | Thee.

4. Thou who wast straitened to be .... | bap - tized | for us!
5. As in the emblem of Thy death we are..... | buried with | Thee,
6. As in the likeness of thy resurrection we are | raised with | Thee,

4. Who didst pass through the deep | waters to re- | deem ... | us!
5. In the fellowship of Thy ...... | sufferings .. | will we | follow Thee.
6. So in union with Thy .... | life may we | live with | Thee.

* The Chant and the Anthem may be performed separately or in connection. When there are several candidates, one verse may be sung at each Baptism.

BAPTISMAL HYMNS. 73

EMBLEM.—CONTINUED.
(ANTHEM. PAGES 73—76.)

BAPTISMAL HYMNS. 77

SELECTIONS OF PASSAGES FOR CHANTING.

The natural relation of the passages included in each of the three following pieces, will be sufficiently obvious without particular remark. The division of sentences, in some instances, into parts of very unequal length, and the occasional transposition of clauses, have been adopted, partly with reference to variety or emphasis of musical expression, and partly for the purpose of securing as much of rhythmical movement as is compatible with an exact representation of the Scriptural declaration. The music, which is by the Rev. R. Lowry, has been very successfully adapted to the arrangement. The repeated change of key indicated in the first of the pieces, as it is naturally demanded by the significancy of the passages, will be introduced with excellent effect.

THEN COMETH JESUS.

R. L.

1 Then cometh Jesus--unto John to be bap - - - | tized of | him.
2 And He went up straightway.................... | out of the | water ;

3 And He saw the Spirit of God de - - - - - | scending like a | dove,
4 And lo, a voice from heaven, saying, This is my be - | lov - ed | Son,
5 And He said,............................. | Thus it be - | cometh us

1 And He was bap - - - - | tized of | him in the | Jordan.
2 And lo, the......................... | heavens were | op - ened | unto Him ;

3 (Omit .... | ....) and | light-ing up- | on Him.
4 In...................................... | whom I am | well........ | pleased.
5 To ful - - - - | fill all | right - eous - | ness.

FATHER OF OUR SPIRITS.

[ADAPTED TO ORDINARY OCCASIONS OF PUBLIC WORSHIP.]

(Chant on page 77.)
    Father of our spirits! as with | thankful | penitence,—
    In witness, that, bathing us in the | fountain | of Thy | love,
    Thou hadst buried from Thy remembrance | our in- | iquities,—
    In the baptismal | waters | we did con- | fess Thee,
    So would we now, by Thy grace, in remembrance | of our | vows,
    Yield ourselves joyfully to Thee, and | thankful- | ly o- | bey Thee.

(1st Chant on the preceding page.—Minor key.)
    Thou who wast straitened to be bap- | tized for | us!
    Who didst pass through the deep | waters | to re- | deem us!
    As in the emblem of Thy death we were | buried | with Thee,
    So in the fellowship of Thy | sufferings | we will | follow Thee:
    As in the likeness of Thy resurrection we were | raised with | Thee,
    So in union with Thy | life may we | live with | Thee.

(2nd Chant on the preceding page.—Major key.)
    Spirit of holiness | and of | truth!
    For Thy life-giving | influence | do we | bless Thee;
    In our weakness we trust Thee and would be | led by | Thee.
    O'erwhelm us with the | fullness | of Thy | grace;
    Baptize us in the | light of Thy | glory,—
    That we may live in | Thee and | walk in | Thee.

(Chant on page 77.)
    And we will serve Thee, the Father, the Son, and the | Holy | Spirit,
    In holiness and righteousness all the | days of our | life. A- | men.

THEN COMETH JESUS.

(Chant on page 77.)
1. Then cometh Jesus--unto John to be bap- | tized of | him.
   And He was bap- | tized of | him in the | Jordan.
2. And He went up straightway | out of the | water;
   And lo, the | heavens were | opened | unto Him;
3. And He saw the Spirit of God de- | scending like a | dove,
   | And | lighting up- | on Him.
4. And lo, a voice from heaven, saying, This is my be- | loved | Son,
   In | whom I am | well | pleased.
5. And He said, | Thus it be- | cometh us
   To ful- | fill all | righteous- | ness.

(1st Chant on the preceding page.—Minor key.)
6. I have a baptism to | be bap- | tized with;
   And how am I straitened, | till it | be ac- | complished!
7. I am come into deep waters where the | floods over- | flow me;
   The waters are come | in un- | to my | soul.
8. I lay down my life, that I may | take it a- | gain.
   I am the resur- | rection | and the | life.
9. He that believeth on me, though he were dead, | yet shall he | live.
   Because | I live, | ye shall live | also.

(2nd Chant on the preceding page.—Major key.)
10. All power is given unto me in | heaven and in | earth:
    Go ye, therefore, | and | teach all | nations.
11. Baptizing them in the | name of the | Father,
    And of the Son, and | of the | Holy | Ghost;
12. Teaching them to observe all things whatsoever | I have com- | manded you:
    And lo, I am with you alway, even unto the | end | of the | world. | A- | men

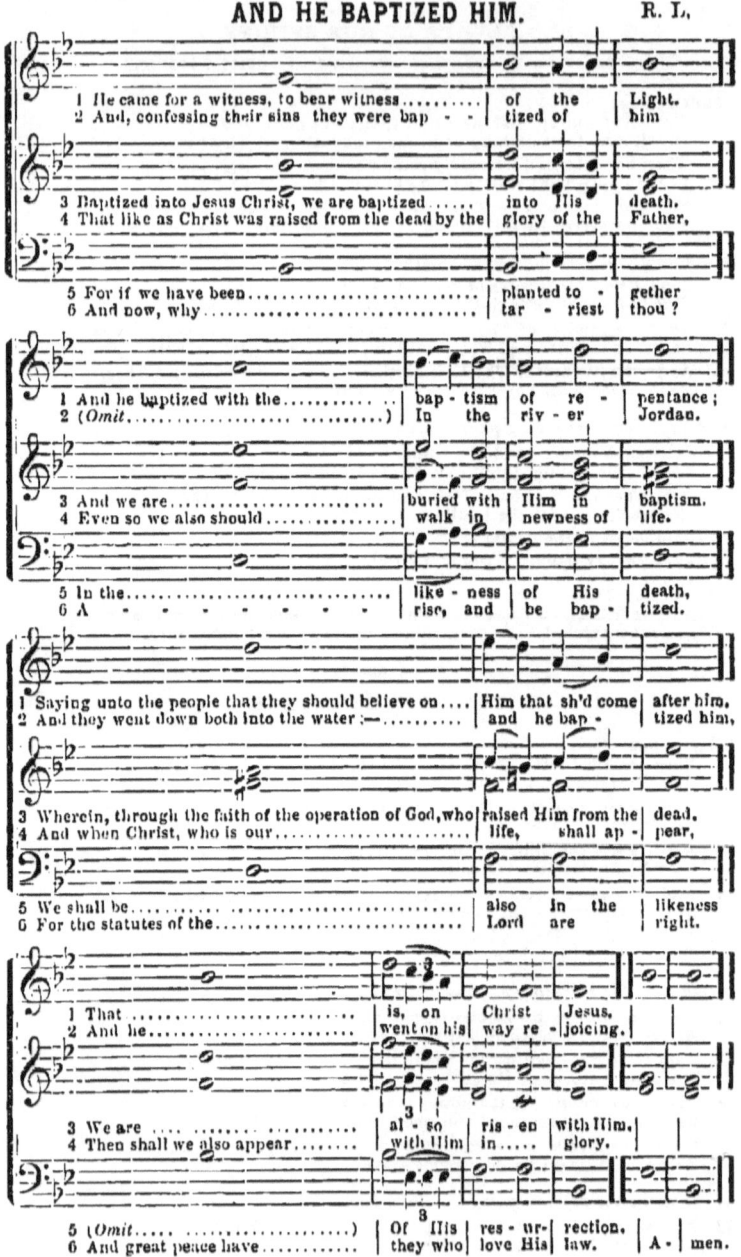

AND HE BAPTIZED HIM.

(A selection of verses will easily be made in cases where it may seem to be desirable.)

1 He came for a witness to bear witness | of the | Light.
And he baptized with the | baptism | of re-| pentance ;
Saying unto the people that they should believe on | Him that should come | after Him
That | is, on | Christ | Jesus.

2 And, confessing their sins, they were bap-| tized of | him
| In the | river | Jordan.
And they went down both into the water :—| and he bap-| tized him.
And he | went on his | way re-| joicing.

3 Baptized into Jesus Christ, we are baptized | into His | death.
We are | buried with | Him in | baptism,
Wherein, through the faith of the operation of God, who | raised Him from the | dead,
We are | also | risen | with Him.—

4 That like as Christ was raised from the dead by the | glory of the | Father,
Even so we also should | walk in | newness of | life.
And when Christ, who is our | life, shall ap-| pear,
Then shall we also appear | with Him | in—| glory.

5 For if we have been | planted to-| gether
In the | likeness | of His | death,
We shall be | also in the | likeness
| Of His | resur-| rection.

6 And now, why | tarriest | thou ?
A-| rise, and | be bap-| tized.
For the statutes of the | Lord are | right ;
And great peace have | they who | love His | law.

7 The judgments of the | Lord are | good ;
They are true and | righteous | alto-| gether.
His commandments | are not | grievous.
And in keeping of them | there is | great re-|ward. | A-| men.

I MADE HASTE AND DELAYED NOT.

See page 82.

1 I made haste and delayed not to | keep — | Thy com-| mandments.
I esteem all Thy precepts concerning | all things | to be | right.
I will delight myself in Thy commandments | which I have | loved.
Teach me the way of Thy statutes ; and I shall | keep it | unto the | end.

2 What shall I render unto the Lord for all His | bene-| fits toward | me ?
I will offer the sacrifices of righteousness, and will | put my | trust in the | Lord.
I will walk in Thy truth ; and I will praise Thee with | all my | heart ;
And I will glorify Thy | name for-| ever-| more.

3 I will pay my vows unto the Lord now in the | presence of | all His | people.
Come and hear, all ye that fear God ; and I will declare what | He hath | done for my | soul.
I will wait on Thy name ; for it is good be-| fore Thy | saints.—
Thy saints that are in the earth, and the excellent, in | whom is ! all my de-| light.

4 I will walk before the Lord in the | land — | of the | living ;
For Thou art the strength of my heart, | and my | portion for-| ever.
Thou shalt guide me with Thy counsel, and afterward re-| ceive me to | glory.
I shall be satisfied, when I a-| wake,—a-| wake, with Thy | likeness. | A-| men.

I MADE HASTE AND DELAYED NOT.

R. L.

1 I made haste and delayed not to .... keep ...... Thy com|mandments,
2 What shall I render unto the Lord for all His|ben - e - |fits toward| me?

3 I will pay my vows unto the Lord now in the|pres-ence of| all His| people.
4 I will walk before the Lord in the .... |land ..... | of the | living.

1 I esteem all Thy precepts concerning .... |all things| to .... be | right.
2 I will offer the sacrifices of righteousness, and will|put my| trust in the| Lord.

3 Come and hear, all ye that fear God; and I will de-
 clare what..|He hath| done for my| soul.
4 For Thou art the strength of my heart,........ |and my| portion for-| ever.

1 I will delight myself in Thy commandments,............|which I have| loved.
2 I will walk in Thy truth; and I will praise Thee with.....|all my| heart;

3 I will wait on Thy name; for it is good be - - - |fore Thy| saints,—
4 Thou shalt guide me with Thy counsel, and afterward re-|ceive me to| glory.

1 Teach me the way of Thy statutes; and
 I shall..|keep it | un - to the| end.
2 And I will glorify Thy..................|name for-|ev - er - |more.

3 Thy saints that are in the earth, and the
 excellent, in........................|whom is| all my de-|light.
4 I shall be satisfied, when I a - - |wake, a-|wake, with Thy|likeness,| A - | men.

INDEX TO HYMNS

ADAPTED ALIKE TO BAPTISMAL AND OTHER OCCASIONS.

A considerable number of the foregoing hymns, relating chiefly to the obligations and facts which are recognized in the profession made in baptism, will be found to be, either in whole, or in most of the stanzas, adapted for use on ordinary occasions of worship, whether social or public. The following Index will be found useful in directing attention to them. See page 2.

Page 25,—as follows.
Risen to live with Christ in God,—
Hast thou meekly owned His name?
Meekly tread the heavenly road,
And thy joy in Him proclaim.

Sweetly, on thy tuneful lyre,
Strike the notes of thankful praise;
Sweetly, with th' angelic choir,
Sing the glory of His grace.

Thus pursue thine upward path,
E'er rejoicing on the way,
Till the day-spring light of faith
Lead thee on to perfect day.

Pages 15, 21, 35 and 39.
(Suitable to accompany explanations of the design and uses of baptism.)

Pages 27, 29, 31 and 15.
(Expostulatory with regard to the duty of those who receive the gospel.)

Page 13.
O'er our whole nature, God of grace,
Assert Thy rightful sway.

Page 35.—verses 1—3.
Oh! there's a power in Jesus' life
To raise the soul from earth to heaven.

Page 41.
Our former hopes are slain,
And buried from our sight.

Pages 51 and 89.
Risen with Christ,—to things above
In our faith aspiring.

Page 53,—verses 2 and 3.
Dead with Him who died for you,
Dead to sin and folly.

Page 55,—as follows.
Spirit of glory and of God,
Descend and fill the place;
Come, Gift Divine, and o'er us shed
The fullness of Thy grace.

Like some o'erwhelming, rushing wind
Come in Thy love and might;
Come like the sun's effulgent rays,
And bathe our souls in light.

As Moses sought the sacred mount,
And dwelt within the cloud,
So into Thee we sink from self
To dwell with Christ in God.

Page 57.
Jesus by Thy precious merit,
Free me from the guilt of sin.

Page 59.
My God, to Thy supreme control
My all I would resign.

Page 61.
Ye know not what ye ask:—
The path to glory lies.

Page 63.
Thus must the glorious Prince of life
All righteousness fulfill.

Page 71.
Baptized in Thy thrice precious name,
Thy blessing, O God, we implore.

Page 73.—Anthem.
Spirit of holiness and of truth.

Pages 71—82.—Chants.
Father of our spirits.
Then cometh Jesus.
I made haste and delayed not.

The two following hymns, relating, the one to the Christian Sabbath, and the other to the Lord's Supper, will be seen to have an obvious connection with the general object proposed in the preparation of the volume. It is hoped they may prove to be an acceptable appendix to the list of baptismal hymns.

SABBATH SONG.

H. M. R. LOWRY.

1. Oh! sweet the hallowed morn
   On which the Savior rose!
   I hail thy quiet dawn,
   Thy calm and blest repose;
   I cast away each worldly care,
   To spend thine hours in praise and pray'r.

2. My heart would fain prolong,
   In accents sweet and loud,
   That primal Sabbath song,
   When all the sons of God,
   In full harmonic concert sang
   His love from whom creation sprang;—

3. Or, in diviner strain,
   With all the heavenly choir,
   The bright, seraphic train,
   Attune anew the lyre
   In praise to Him, our living Head,
   Who rose triumphant from the dead.

4. In sweet and grateful lays,
   I touch the sounding chord;
   I sing His power and grace,—
   I trust His faithful word,—
   Nor doubt His resurrection love
   Will bring me to His rest above.

IN REMEMBRANCE OF ME.

1 O love divine! O matchless grace! Which in this sacred rite Shines forth, so full, so free, in rays Of pure and living light!

2 O wondrous death! O precious blood!
  For us so freely spilt,
To cleanse our sin polluted souls
  From every stain of guilt!

3 O covenant of life and peace!
  By blood and suffering sealed!
All the rich gifts of gospel grace
  Are here to faith revealed.

4 Jesus, we bow our souls to Thee,
  Our Life, our Hope, our All,
While we, with thankful, contrite hearts,
  Thy dying love recall.

5 Oh! may Thy pure and perfect laws
  Be written on our minds,
Nor earth, nor self, nor sin obscure
  The ever radiant lines.

KENDRICK.

S. M. See page 41.   C. Hatch Smith.

1. Our for-mer hopes are slain, And bu-ried from our sight; Raised to a new and heaven-ly life, We trace the path of light.

2 Up from the sacred flood,
  Rejoicing in our Head,
 We rise in witness of the power
  Which raised Him from the dead.

3 With lively hope we wait
  The resurrection day;
 We press to reach the promised prize,
  Rejoicing on our way.

GANO.

8s. See page 23. R. LOWRY.

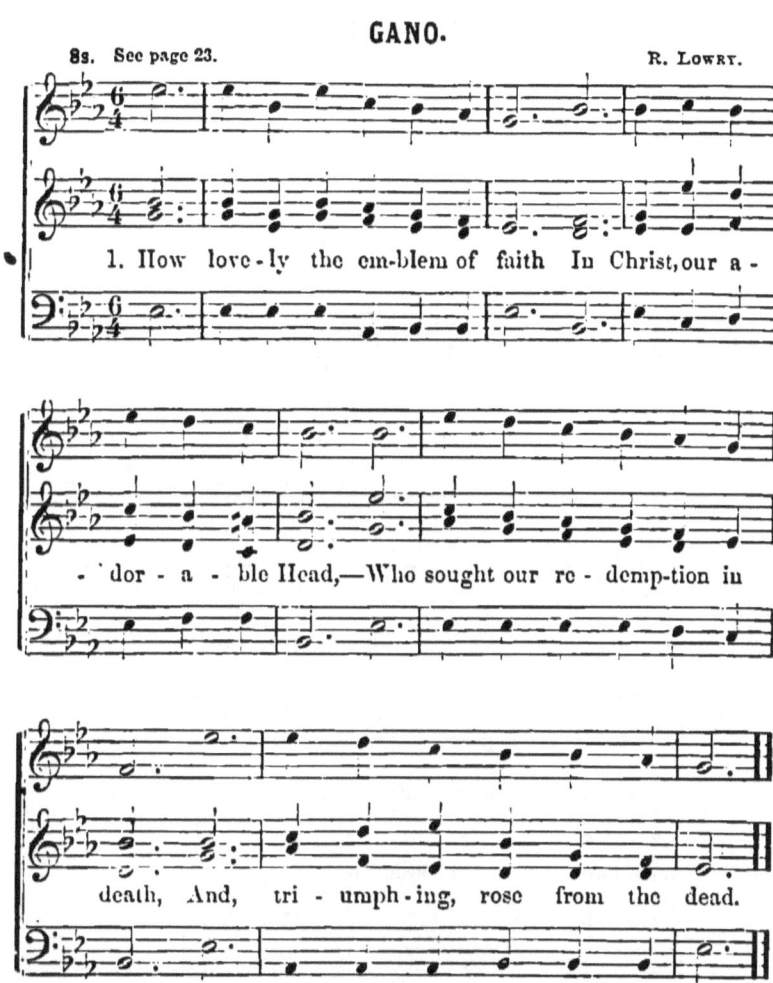

1. How lovely the emblem of faith In Christ, our adorable Head,—Who sought our redemption in death, And, triumphing, rose from the dead.

2.
How sweet in this beautiful rite
  Our union with Him to proclaim,—
Our death to each sinful delight,—
  Our rising to life through His name.

3.
How blessed, by bearing the cross,
  To show our regard for His will,—
To seek, while professing His cause,
  'All righteousness thus to fulfill.'

4.
How pleasant the path to pursue
  His perfect example has led ;
With th' scene at the Jordan in view,
  We haste in His footsteps to tread.

5.
Dear Savior, Thine ordinance bless ;
  The joy of Thy presence make known;
Descend, O Thou Spirit of grace,
  And seal us for ever thine own.

BAPTISMAL HYMNS.

The following excellent piece of music has been kindly furnished by its author for the words which are here printed with it, and from which it is allowed to take its name. It is not published, however, as a constituent part of this volume. It is inserted as by permission from proof sheets of "The Sabbath School Cluster."

GLORY IN FRUITION.

1 Risen with Christ,—to things a-bove In our faith as-pir-ing, In the ar-dor of our hope Him a-lone de-sir-ing,—We will walk as 'pilgrims here,'

2 With Him in His dy-ing love Still in sweet com-mun-ion, To His re-sur-rec-tion life Joined in clos-est un-ion, We will spurn the world's control,

3 Faith that glo-ry shall re-veal To our rap-tured vis-ion, Till shall burst up-on our view Glo-ry in fru-i-tion,—Till, re-leased from toil and strife,

GLORY IN FRUITION.—CONCLUDED.

BAPTISMAL HYMNS. 91

ROBINS.

The following tune,---of which the melody is by the author of the volume,---has been added since the plates for the preceding pages were finished.

Adagio, Aff. Dolce. Arrangement by C. HATCH SMITH.

1 Ye know not what ye ask:— The path to
2 Your way-ward hearts must learn.... How vain is
3 Your souls must oft be plunged.. Beneath the

glo - ry lies.... A - long the rough and thor - ny
all be - low,... As oft up-on your lips is
swell - ing flood,.. Till from that dark bap-tis - mal

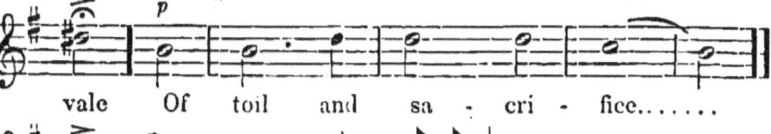

vale Of toil and sa - cri - fice......
pressed The cup of keen - est woe......
stream Ye rise to live for God,—

Find the 4th and 5th stanzas on page 61.   See Note on page 100.

Index of First Lines.

	No. Hymn.	of page. Tunes.
Baptized in Thy thrice precious name,	71, 83	71, 22, 87, 38
Beside this placid pool,	45,	44, 84.
Dead with Him who died for you,—2d v.	53, 83	52.
Didst Thou, O spotless Son of God,	15.	14, 85 70, 58, 36, 54
Didst thou tell me of the Savior,	47.	46, 56,
His kingdom shall ever increase,	39.	38 & 40, 22, 71, 87
How lovely the emblem of faith	23.	22, 87 18, 38, 71
How precious this memorial sign,	37.	36, 14, 54, 70, 58, 85
In the joy of the Spirit,	49.	48 & 50
I will walk, in the joy of my Lord,	19.	18, 22, 38 & 40, 87, 71
Jesus, by Thy precious merit,	57, 83	56, 46
Jesus, we love this sacred rite,	43.	42, 26, 16, 34
Meekly from the mystic flood,	25, 83	24
My God, to Thy supreme control,	59, 83	58, 36, 70, 14, 54, 85
Not still on Calvary's brow,	33.	32, 20, 60, 30, 86
O'er our whole nature, God of grace,	13, 70	70, 36, 58, 14, 85, 54
Oh! sweet the hallowed morn,	84,	84, 44
Oh! sweet the sacred sign	21.	20, 32, 30, 86, 60
Oh! there's a power in Jesus' life,	35, 83	34, 26, 16, 42
Oh! there's a voice in this blest rite,	17,	16, 88, 34, 26, 42
O love divine! O matchless grace!	85,	85, 14, 54, 36, 58, 70
Once more resounds the heavenly word,	29.	30
Our former hopes are slain,	41, 83	86, 20, 32, 30, 60
Put on the Lord—If thou hast known,	27.	26, 34, 42, 16
Risen to live with Christ in God,	83.	24
Risen with Christ,—to things above,	51, 83	89 & 90, 52
Spirit of glory and of God,	55, 83	54, 58, 85, 70, 14, 36
Spirit of holiness and of truth,—Anthem,	73.	73—76
Thus must the glorious Prince of life,	63, 83	62, 64 & 65, 66—69
Welcome from the whelming wave,	53.	52
Why linger on the brink,	31.	30, 32, 20, 86, 60
Ye know not what ye ask,	61, 83	60, 32, 20. 30, 86

CHANTS.

Father of our spirits,	72, 79	72, 77 & 78
And he baptized him,	81.	80
I made haste and delayed not,	81.	82
Then cometh Jesus,	79,	77 & 78

Index to Tunes.

Meter	Tune	Composer	Page
L. M.	Granville,	Wm. B. Bradbury	26
	Judson,	C. Hatch Smith	16
	Mayville	T. E. Perkins	34
	Radiance,	C. W. Smith	88
	Utica,	R. Lowry	42
C. M.	Aspiration,	Wm. B. Bradbury	58
	Bunyan,	C. Hatch Smith	14
	Cincinnati,	Wm. B. Bradbury	70
	In remembrance of me,	C. Hatch Smith	85
	Rippon,	J. R. Osgood	36
	Taylor,	C. Hatch Smith	54
S. M.	Eastville,	Wm. B. Bradbury	60
	Hanson Place,	R. Lowry	32
	Hartford,	C. Hatch Smith	20
	Kendrick,	do.	86
	Stillman,	do.	30
H. M.	Hamilton,	R. Lowry	44
	Sabbath Song,	do.	84
C. H. M.	Acceptance,	T. E. Perkins	62
	Gillette,	C. W. Smith	64, 65
8s, 6s & 4s.	Conquest,	Geo. F. Root	28
7s.	Dayspring,	C. W. Smith	24
8s & 7s	Herbertsville,	C. Hatch Smith	56
	Stennett,	R. Lowry	46
7s & 6s.	Glory in Fruition,	Wm. M. Little	89, 90
7s, 6s & 8s.	The Church's Welcome,	Geo. F. Root	52
8s.	Doxology,	M. Colburn	71
	Gano,	R. Lowry	87
	Sarles,	C. Hatch Smith	22
8s or 9s.	Stratfield,	Geo. F. Root	38, 40
	Talcott,	T. E. Perkins	18
7s, 6s & 5s.	Olive,	J. R. Osgood	48, 50

ANTHEMS.

Tune	Composer	Page
Emblem,	C. Hatch Smith	73—76
The Twofold Baptism,	Geo. F. Root	66—69

CHANTS.

Tune	Composer	Page
Emblem,	C. Hatch Smith	72
And he baptized him,	R. Lowry	80
I made haste and delayed not,	do.	82
Then cometh Jesus,	do.	77, 78

Tunes in common use.

The following list of names of tunes, most of which are in common use, will be found convenient in selecting appropriate music for the several hymns, in cases where the original tunes are not used.

PAGE.
13 Dundee, Cambridge, Piety, Mear, York.
15 Windsor, Naomi, Siloam, Arlington, Woodland.
17 Migdol, Zephyr, Luton, Hartell.
19 Union Hymn, Hunter.
21 Dennis, Golden Hill, St. Michael, Leslie.
23 De Fleury, Foster.
25 Hendon, Pleyel's Hymn, Benevento, Nuremberg, Horton.
27 Hebron, Rockingham, Evening Hymn, Missionary Chant.
31 Olmutz, State Street, Olney, Paddington.
33 Shirland, Shawmut, Watchman, Hereford.
35 Federal Street, Mendon, Duke Street, Bridgewater.
37 Azmon, St. Martins, Devizes, Ortonville, Stephens.
39 Madison, Adnal, Confidence.
41 Silver Street, St. Thomas, Badea, Laban.
43 Ward, Winchester, Hamburg, Uxbridge.
45 Haddam, Zebulon, Amherst, Flanders.
47 Autumn, Worthing, Sicilian Hymn, Jaynes,
49 Portuguese Hymn. Goshen. Hanover, Frederick.
55 Evan, Peterboro, Dedham, Hermon, Northfield.
57 Greenville, Vesper Hymn, Wilmot, Sardius.
59 Brown, Downs, Cross and Crown, New York Tune.
61 Boylston, Aylesbury, Hartland, Thatcher.
63 Calm, Orgel, Watch and Pray.

NOTES OF REFERENCE

TO THE PRECEDING PAGES.

The following Notes are inserted as an addition to the original plan of the volume. As they relate, for the most part, to important doctrinal and practical uses and relations of baptism, which either did not come within the range of discussion in the Introduction, or which at best could there be stated with less distinctness and specialty of application or exposition than as here presented, it is hoped they will be found to be an appropriate and useful supplement to the work.

Note 1.—*Page* 13.

"*O'er our whole nature.*"—A proper profession of a personal connection with the kingdom of Christ, does not relate simply to the forgiveness of sins, or a passive reception of spiritual blessings. It has respect not less to the experience of a spiritual *change* which extends to the whole conscious activity of the subject, involving, on the one hand, the bringing of the whole being into subjection "to the obedience of Christ," and, on the other, the conscious, active yielding of all the living powers to His will and Spirit.

Nor can we assume that this feature of the Christian profession is incidental, or to be learned by implication from the analogy of faith. It is essentially and specially characteristic. It is indicated as such in the very nature of the work of redemption. That which the subject is supposed, in obedience to the Spirit, and in the exercise of a joyous faith, to have yielded to Christ, as having been redeemed by Him, is expressly and distinctively his "whole" being.—1 Thess. 5: 23; 1 Cor. 6: 11, 14, 20; Rom. 6: 13; 2 Tim. 1: 10, 12: 2: 8—11, 18.

To this aspect of the real nature of a suitable Christian profession, there is a perfect adaptation in the significancy of Christian *baptism*. This is seen in what is necessarily involved in its proper symbolical import as related to a union with Christ in His death and resurrection. In passing beneath the baptismal waters, as one who is "buried with Christ," the subject signifies that he has by the Spirit given himself up unreservedly to the influence of the death of Christ in its relation to the destruction of sin in his nature; while in his rising again, as one who has "risen with Christ," he has in symbol a gracious pledge that what he has yielded to Christ, will be "preserved" by Him unto the glory which is to be revealed, at His "coming," in "the resurrection at the last day."—1 Thess. 5: 23; Col. 3: 1—4; John 6: 39, 40; 1 Pet. 1: 3—5. Of this consummation, baptism is, in fact, a most instructive representation and prophecy.

NOTE 2.—*Page* 17.

"*Which far beyond the power of speech.*"—The hymn on the 17th page, was first sung on the occasion of the baptism by the writer of one who, while deaf and dumb, had seemed especially to appreciate the intrinsic significance and impressiveness of the ordinance, as adapted to show forth the death and resurrection of the Lord Jesus. It is entirely appropriate, however, to any ordinary occasion of baptism.

It is worthy of notice, that in the symbolical ordinances of the gospel, Christ is presented to view only in His union with His people. In baptism, His death and resurrection are represented in the burial and rising again of those who are "buried with Him." This identification of a recognition of the great facts of His work of mediation, with whatever is solemn and affecting in a personal and formal profession of the gospel, is doubtless adapted, more than any merely verbal statement, to leave a most pleasing impression of their preciousness and power on the depths of the Christian's consciousness.

NOTE 3.—*Page* 21.

"*And raised to share His glorious life.*—The great blessing of the gospel is LIFE, John 3: 16, life through death to the past, 2 Tim. 2: 11, and this as the fruit of the mediation of Christ. In its realization, it is, even as here enjoyed by the Christian, an actual communion with Him in the blessedness of His own glorious resurrection life.—Col. 3: 1—3. It accordingly becomes the sure pledge and earnest of its own perfection. In being, in connection with a living faith, "quickened with Christ," we have the assurance, not only that we shall live with Him in glory, but that even our "mortal bodies" which are destined to be "sown in corruption," shall be "raised in incorruption," "fashioned like unto His glorious body.' How impressive the ordinance appointed to show forth this life, and the union of the believer with its source!

NOTE 4.—*Page* 27.

"*In glad obedience to His word.*"—As baptism is in its very design a *profession* of faith in the Lord Jesus Christ, and of submission to His gospel, Col, 2: 12, so is it simply impossible that what has not yet been consciously experienced, should be consciously and properly professed. Submission to the rite, like the profession which it represents, is necessarily a personal duty. The service belongs to no one as a birth-right inheritance. As "that which is born of the flesh, is flesh" without distinction of parental descent, so "that which is born of the Spirit, is spirit" by a process which recognizes no considerations of natural relationship, and is adapted solely to the *common necessity* of a fallen and sinful nature.

Wherever there is a consciousness of this common experience, relating to deliverance from a common sinful state, it is obviously fit that it should have some *common* formal expression. Such an expression the gospel supplies in *baptism*. It is the appointed rite for acknowledging the new relationship and the conscious experience which evinces it. And submission to it *as such* is the common right and privilege and duty of those who, while equally destitute of all claims arising from hereditary relations, have, "according to God's abundant *mercy*," obtained a "like precious faith," and been "begotten again" to the enjoyment of the same "lively hope." They may rejoice in the assurance that there is for them, *as* the grateful subjects of this new experience, "one Lord, one faith, one baptism."

The Christian church, relating properly as an organization to such only as give evidence that they have believed to the saving of the soul, Acts 2: 47, and that they will be finally acknowledged as "redeemed from among men," is not, like the Hebrew commonwealth, a national community. The relations which it represents are not hereditary or natural, but spiritual. It invites to its membership such only as give indication that they have, by God's own special agency, Col. 1: 12, 13, made obvious by their "love in the Spirit,"Col. 1: 8, been "translated " from a previous state of sin, "*into* the kingdom of His dear Son." Aside from the evidence of this " translation," in such indications as are stated in John 1 : 12, 13; Acts 26: 20; Rom. 14: 17, there can be no proper basis for Christian fellowship or its recognition as relating to a " new life " in Christ Jesus.

One of the strongest incentives to faithful labor in behalf of the objects of Christian responsibility, is supplied by a proper appreciation of this common necessity as existing in the case of those who do not evince that, as "born of the Spirit," they are "spiritual."

Note 5.—*Page* 33.

" *Not still on Calvary's brow.*"—We may suppose that the execution by our Lord of His fearful predictions respecting " the desolations of Jerusalem," during the period in which it was in the possession of the persecutors of His people, was not without some special design with regard to the purpose to be served by the institutions which He had left as the proper memorials of His work, in connection with a fuller appreciation, by His disciples of all lands, of their common privileges, in their union with Him as their living Savior.

The "burial with Christ" involved in baptism, reminds us of His burial in our behalf, not through the medium of a local and vacant sepulchre, but by presenting Him to view directly in His relation to the present experience and hope of those who have been "quickened together with Him." His passage through the tomb is thus brought to our grateful contemplation in a manner the most favorable for the inspiring of an earnest and practical faith and devotion; and "wheresoever in the whole world the gospel is preached," and believers are added to the Lord, there may the full benefit of this impressive remembrancer be enjoyed.

Note 6.—*Page* 37.

"*For a memorial for ever.*"—As in the "one baptism" of the gospel, the subject is, in a significant emblem, presented to view as "RISEN WITH CHRIST," Col. 2: 12, and as the rite, as thus inseparable from this significancy, is enjoined, in the great commission, to be observed "even unto the end of the world," it must necessarily remain, wherever the commission is fulfilled, a perpetual memorial of His resurrection, and a most impressive declaration and witness of the continued participation of His people in the power and blessedness of His resurrection life. Nor is it a matter of indifference, or of personal preference merely, that its testimony in this respect should be withheld from the "nations" to whom the "gospel" is "preached," Matt. 28: 18–20; Mark 16: 15, 16; John 12: 23–28; or that those who become "disciples" or "believers," should be denied the benefits pertaining to an identification of its significancy with their conscious obedience and public character.

Note 7.—*Page* 39.

"*As the Judge of the quick and the dead.*"—The ordinance of baptism belongs, appropriately, from its very significancy, to those who are "risen with Christ." But in testifying to the direct union of His believing people with Him in His resurrection life, it not less clearly, by proclaiming to the world the *fact* of His glorious resurrection, calls attention to the divinely appointed "assurance" that, as "Head over all things to the church," He will appear as "the

Judge of the quick and the dead."—Acts 17: 31. It is especially with reference to the great purposes pertaining to His mediatorial office, that "all power" is recognized in Matt. 28: 18, as "given unto Him in heaven and in earth," while the mysterious personal union of His divine and human nature, as God manifested in the flesh, "in whom are hid all the treasures of wisdom and knowledge," and by whom "all things consist," assures us that His power is supreme and unlimited for "judgment" as well as for blessing.—John 5: 21–27; 1: 1–5, 14; Col. 2: 3, 9; Phil. 3: 21. In connection with His final commission, enjoining that those who "believe" should be "baptized," is the significant declaration that "he that believeth not shall be damned." And the resurrection of the "unjust," or of "those who have done evil" instead of "good," will be, not "in the likeness of His resurrection," but equally with the punishment indicated in Luke 16: 23–31, in fulfillment of this authoritative declaration of His "word."—John 5: 29. He will come to be "glorified in His saints," in "all them who believe," 2 Thess. 1: 10, in them who love Him, 1 Cor. 16: 22, who are accepted in Him, Eph. 1: 6, who have been quickened together with Him.—Col. 3: 4.

NOTE 8.—*Page* 41.

"*In hope of the glory of God.*"—The final inheritance of those who, "led by the Spirit," are "sons of God," and "joint heirs with Christ," will be received in connection with "the redemption," that is, the resurrection and glorification of the "body," whereby the power of death over their nature will be completely and finally destroyed, 1 Cor. 15: 26, 54, and a conformity to the image of Him who is the Firstborn among many brethren, in the full glory of His resurrection state, will be attained.—Rom. 8: 17–19, 29. In their spiritual existence and consciousness, however, they are, even in this world, partakers of the life of Christ, "quickened" and "raised up with Him," Eph. 2: 5, 6; Rom. 6: 4–13; 8: 10; Col. 3: 1–3; and this union, once enjoyed, is, in its very nature, perpetual.—John 5: 24; 11: 26. As those who may "kill the body," are "not able to kill the soul," Matt. 10: 28, still less, if possible, can they reach the spiritual life and more perfect felicity of those who are "absent from the body," only that they may be "present with the Lord."—2 Cor. 5: 7, 8; 12: 2–4; Phil. 1: 20–23. Of Him "the whole family in heaven and earth is named;" and He is now, no less than He will be when His glory is more fully "manifested" or "revealed in them," their common "Head."—Heb. 12: 23; Eph. 1: 22; 3: 15; Col. 1: 12.

Note 9.—*Page* 53.

"*Welcome to our happy band.*"—The hymn on the 53rd page, may be appropriately sung, either in immediate connection with the administration of the ordinance, as an expression of welcome from the church to the subject, as he rises from the water, or as an accompaniment to the subsequent address of the pastor.

The relation of a voluntary submission to baptism to a recognition of membership in the primitive churches, is equally apparent from the Acts of the apostles, and the apostolic epistles. The members of these churches are, as often as occasion requires, expressly and familiarly recognized and described as those who had been "buried with Christ in baptism," and who therein had testified "the answer of a good conscience toward God," 1 Pet. 3 : 21, in connection with their "faith" in the gospel, Col. 2 : 12, their attainment to "newness of life," and their purpose to "walk" therein.—Rom. 6 : 4.

Note 10.—*Page* 55.

"*And Moses went into the midst of the cloud.*"—The conception of an *immersion* in the symbol of the Divine presence and holiness, enjoyed as a token of special favor, could hardly fail to be familiar to the minds of those who were conversant with the history of God's ancient people. See 1 Cor. 10 : 1, 2. Compare also Luke 9 : 34; Matt. 17 : 5; 2 Pet. 1 : 17. This representation would naturally, in accordance with the established usages of language, pass over from the symbol to that which was symbolized. See 1 Pet. 4 : 14; 2 Cor. 3 : 8; Mark 1 : 8. Compare also John 3 : 8, and Acts 2 : 2.

Note 11.—*Page* 61.

"*Ye rise to live for God.*"—It is a just occasion for "joy" to the Christian, Jas. 1 : 2–4, that his "chastening," although, "for the present, grievous," is, nevertheless, designed for his "profit," and will, if rightly received, yield to him "the peaceable fruit of righteousness;" that, however deep and overwhelming the trials and afflictions he may experience in his "striving against sin," in the disappointment of his earthly hopes, or by the special allotments of Providence, he may cherish the conviction, that, in yielding to their proper "working," Rom. 5 : 3–5, he is passing through them only that he may *emerge* from them into a higher state of light and joy and "holiness," Heb. 12 : 10, and to a fuller appreciation of his spiritual relations and privileges.

Note. 11—*Page 63.*

"*Till, dead to self and sin's control.*"—The more fully we bring our own grateful feelings into sympathy with the experience of our Lord in His submersion in death for us, the more readily will they, not only become heartily reconciled, were it necessary, to the form of the rite which He has appointed as a sign of our fellowship with Him, but be brought into positive and most lively sympathy with its fullest import.

It is a fact which we may not disregard, that, as often as our Lord, in the course of His ministry, takes occasion to call attention to the idea of "baptism" as related to Himself, He presents it in such a light that we necessarily conceive of it as realized in what is expressed in *the simple, characteristic meaning of the word.* His immersion in the Jordan was not with reference to a cleansing as any part of its significancy. No such idea is associated with the performance of the act. And yet it was, in the proper religious application of the term, a real, a characteristic, a perfect baptism. It was ever to remain in the gospel history, as suggesting the essential idea expressed by the word as it should be familiarly used by His disciples. Nor was it an empty form. It was a baptism full of most interesting and precious import.

We solicit attention to the light in which this identification of the rite in its observance with the act of the Master, has presented it for our contemplation. Is there nothing suggestive in the fact that He has placed at the very commencement of His public ministry, such an exhibition of baptism as compels us, not only to recognize the distinctive idea which the word suggests, in the specific act which it properly expresses, but to find its very significancy, as thus exhibited, *in Himself?* Or is it less significant that the same relation of facts should be repeatedly recalled to notice in His subsequent teaching, by references to "baptism" in connection with allusions to His final sufferings?—Mark. 10: 38; Luke 12: 50. "Are ye able to be baptized with the baptism that I am baptized with?" "I have a baptism to be baptized with: and how am I straitened till it be accomplished!" The idea of *overwhelming* or *submersion,* which established usage had inseparably united in familiar thought with the word whenever applied, as in these passages, to what were in reality overwhelming sufferings, and which it would be impossible for the disciples, even if they would, to separate from it, unites itself with a natural and obvious reference to His immersion in the Jordan; and we are reminded that the latter was but an emblem and prophecy of a submersion in death which was yet to be experienced, and the depth and fearfulness of which can be estimated only by a knowledge of the character and relations of the Subject.

Such is the conception of baptism which necessarily results from the proper contemplation of its relation to Him who was "baptized" for us. As we stand at the baptismal pool, awaiting baptism "in *His* name," and follow Him in our faith and sympathy and love, as for us He passes beneath the dark billows of death, with all its elements of humiliation, and suffering, and ignominy, and wrath as manifested against sin, gathering over Him, till we see Him rise again to a glorious life, the idea of "baptism" as thus exemplified, becomes consecrated in our hearts. With the feelings thus awakened, we would not, even were it possible, separate from the meaning of the word in its relation to our own profession, what is thus recognized as being at once its proper, characteristic sense, and the only sense in which it could in any view have an application to Him who is the Author and Object of our faith. We feel that the act of passing beneath the baptismal flood in obedience to His appointment, in token of our fellowship with Him in the design of His death, is but a slight expression of our gratitude for the "baptism" which He endured for us.

It was impossible that this conception of the nature and relations of baptism should not have been perpetually present to the minds of the early Christians in their observance of the rite. With the history of their Savior's immersion in the Jordan, as it is recorded by the evangelists, and His own repeated allusions to the "baptism" which He was to undergo, as associated with the predictions of His death, continually before them, and incorporated with their most cherished remembrance of the righteousness which He had fulfilled in their behalf, they could not, even had they desired, have failed to compare the idea of baptism as thus exemplified in the example and experience of the Master, with its application to the case of the disciple. It becomes no occasion for surprise that we find the apostle, in writing to the Christians at Rome and at Colosse, as to those who had "not seen his face in the flesh," assuming that the fact that as many as were baptized into Jesus Christ, were "baptized into His death," and "buried with Him in baptism," was one which was within their familiar knowledge, and had actually been recognized in their own baptism; and that it was only necessary for him to *apply* it to the enforcement and elucidation of the truth which he would commend to their regard, and to bring more fully and explicitly to their apprehension its real practical bearings. His manner in introducing these allusions is in all respects as natural, and comes as entirely within the range of what we might have anticipated, as when, with a view to the practical application and improvement of the fact, he urges upon the earnest consideration of the Christians at Corinth, what he himself had once "delivered to them," and which we may believe was universally recognized among the primitive churches, and needed only to be stated to be admitted, to wit, that the elements employed in the ordinance of the Supper, were, by the very nature of the rite, designed to have a sacred commemorative and symbolical reference to "the body and blood of the Lord."—1 Cor. 11: 27. Compare verses 20—26.

Such a view of baptism in its relations to the death of Christ, prepares us, as it did the early disciples, to appreciate its significancy in its relation to an experience which is identified with His resurrection life, and which becomes manifest to our consciousness and to the world, by all those evidences of holy joy and faith and hope and living energy, which are the natural fruit of such a relationship. "Except a corn of wheat fall into the ground and die. it abideth alone; but *if it die*, it bringeth forth much fruit."

Note 12.—*Page* 83.

"*To dwell with Christ in God.*"—The distinctive office work of the Holy Spirit, in His enlightening and transforming influence, is to *bring the soul into fellowship with Christ*, in the design of His death as endured for the destruction of sin, and in the realization of the blessedness of His glorious resurrection life.

It is the explicit declaration accompanying the promise of the gift of the Spirit,—"He shall glorify me."—"He shall testify of me."—"He shall take of mine, and shall show it unto you."—John 16: 14, 15; 15: 26. The things, pertaining to the work of Christ, which are "freely given to us of God," are "revealed unto us by His Spirit."—1 Cor. 2: 10, 12. By the renewing of the Holy Spirit, we are made "new creatures" "in Christ."—Eph. 2: 10; 2 Cor. 5: 17. By the sanctification of the Spirit, we are "sanctified in Christ Jesus."—1 Cor. 1: 12. Indeed, it is "Christ" who, by the powerful agency of the Spirit, is made unto us "sanctification," no less than "wisdom, and righteousness and redemption."—1 Cor. 1: 24, 30.; 6: 11; 2 Cor. 3: 18. In Christ we are "builded together for a habitation of God, through the Spirit."—Eph. 2: 22. Our bodies, as the "members of Christ," are the temples of the Holy Spirit.—1 Cor. 6; 11, 15, 19.

As, on the one hand, it is "through the Spirit" that we are enabled to "mortify," or, more exactly, *put to death*, "the deeds of the body," as those who are "dead with Christ," Rom. 8: 13; 6: 8; so, on the other, it is the Spirit, as "the Spirit of *life*," that brings us into union with the resurrection life of Christ.—Rom. 8: 2—11. While the body is "dead, because of sin," it is by the Spirit, imparting to us His life-giving influence, that our spirit becomes "life, because of righteousness;"

and this as a proof that "Christ" is in us.—Rom. 8: 9, 10. Indeed, we have, in the indwelling of "the Spirit of Him who raised up Jesus from the dead," the assurance that even our mortal bodies shall be quickened, and made like unto His glorious body.—Rom. 8: 11, 23, 17; Phil. 3: 21. The Spirit, by His life-giving power made obvious in its operation to our consciousness, becomes to us the "earnest" of our inheritance, as "joint heirs with Christ," or the "firstfruits" of our "glorification with Him," Rom. 8: 23, 17; a glorification which will be consummated in our final "adoption, to wit, the redemption of our body."—Rom. 8: 17—30. Compare Gal. 6: 8; 3: 1—3; Eph. 1: 13, 14; 4: 30; 2 Cor. 5: 5.

In beautiful harmony with this representation of the office work and witness of the Holy Spirit, appears the witness involved in the emblematical significancy of baptism. It relates not so much to the secret operation of the Spirit in His enlightening, convincing, renewing, sanctifying, strengthening, witnessing, life-giving, indwelling influence, as to the blessed *results* thereby attained in a real union of the soul with Christ. The design of the rite is to exhibit the work of the Spirit, in its reality and glory, *as accomplished*, rather than any hidden, spiritual process by which the result is reached. As it pertains to the special object of the Spirit's agency in the work of redemption, to "glorify Christ," as God manifested in the flesh, and the "one Mediator between God and men," it is obvious that wherever a soul is brought into *fellowship with Christ* in His death for the destruction of sin, and in the all pervading power and blessedness of His resurrection life, there is exhibited, in accomplishment, THE WORK OF THE SPIRIT. And the Spirit Himself is honored, as he could be by no other formal act, in the proper recognition and acknowledgement of this result, in the significant profession of union with Christ in His death and resurrection life, which is made in Christian baptism.

In the mediation of Christ, as accomplished in His own person, are a death for sin, and the ever present power of a glorious mediatorial resurrection life.—Heb. 9: 26; 7: 25. In the work of the Spirit are a death to sin, and a life to righteousness, on the part of those who become united to Christ, Rom. 8: 13, 9—11, involving a resurrection with Christ to newness of life and to a "living hope" of final glorification with Him.—Rom. 6: 4, 5; 8: 1—11; 15; 13; 1 Pet: 1: 3. etc. In the significancy of baptism, these, each in its appropriate light, are equally represented in a single act of profession, as being united and inseparable in their relation to the state and experience of the subject.

APPENDIX.

BAPTISM AS A SIGNIFICANT PROFESSION OF THE GOSPEL.

One of the most interesting aspects of baptism is presented in the natural relation to its symbolical import, of the threefold reference in the Christian profession expressed in Mat. 28: 19. In connection with a brief indication of the nature of this relationship, beyond what is noticed on pages 103 and 104, a few additional suggestions with respect to baptism as a significant profession of the gospel and a witness to its truth, may not be inappropriate as related to the contents of the volume in the preceding pages. The facts suggested are commended to the reader's earnest consideration.

"*Baptized in Thy thrice precious name.*"— *Page* 71.— Christ, especially in those aspects of His work which are represented in baptism, appears as the Way to the Father. By this way, in the experience of a living union with Christ, we are brought into an actual relationship of favor and communion with the Father, by the renewing and life-giving influence of the Holy Spirit. From a previous state of separation and estrangement, we "come to the Father," as "led by the Spirit," along the pathway, so to speak, of a *mediatorial* life, which, while in personal union with divinity, on the one hand, and humanity, on the other, represents and possesses the infinite merit of a *finished* work of expiation and righteousness through an "obedience unto death," and becomes to us, by an ever present living energy, the actual source of "all spiritual blessings." See Eph. 1: 3. He who is described in the prophecies announcing His birth, as being "from of old, from everlasting," Mi. 5: 2, 3; Isa. 9: 6, is also, as "the Head of the body, the church," "the First-born from the dead," Col. 1: 17, 18. See also Eph. 1: 19—23; 1 Pet. 3: 21, 22; Mat. 28: 18. It is in anticipation of a resurrection with Him "in glory," that, in becoming united with Him as the members of His body, we are "quickened together with Him," in connection with the "forgiveness of all trespasses," and the exercise of "the faith of the operation of God, who raised Him from the dead."— Col. 1: 27; 3: 4; 2: 12, 13; Eph. 2: 1—6. "The Spirit of Christ," "the Spirit of life," "the Spirit of

Him who raised up Jesus from the dead," is to those who are led by Him, "*the Spirit of adoption*," Rom. 8: 9, 2, 11, 14, 15;—an adoption the witness of which is given in connection with the operation of that life-giving influence which, in the very exercise of it, constitutes them "joint *heirs* with Christ," and which shall be finally "manifested" in connection with the redemption of the body.—Rom. 8: 1—17, 23, 29, 30. It is thus, while they are in conscious union with the resurrection life of Christ, that "God sends forth the SPIRIT of His SON into their hearts, crying, Abba, FATHER." It is precisely at this point that we perceive more clearly, perhaps, than at any other, as if by the concentrated rays of divine truth, how immanent in the whole Christian system, is the doctrine of the Trinity. It is as Christ, the Word who was made flesh, in whom dwells all the fullness of the Godhead bodily, is presented to our view as the First-born from the dead, with His sacrifice accepted, ever living to make intercession, recognized as the Source and Dispenser of all spiritual blessing, the Head and Author of the new relationship implied in the witness of our adoption, and the pledge of our own glorious resurrection and manifestation as the sons of God, that we apprehend, in their most precious connection with our conscious experience and life and hope, the offices and respective relations of "the Father, the Son and the Holy Spirit." And this, as we have seen, is precisely the connection in which they are exhibited in the *symbolical* significancy of baptism.

Dead to sin and the law by the body of Christ! Quickened together with Him! Risen with Him! That we may be glorified with Him! Is there an aspect of Christian privilege or of Christian life, in which appear so fully or shine forth so brightly the distinctive features of the scheme of redemption, as in this simple, comprehensive description of what is emblematically represented in baptism? Where, within the record of inspired teaching, shall we find language so suggestive of all that is precious in the distinguishing doctrines of the gospel, or the experience of its subjects? And is nothing lost to the believer, in his apprehension of the gospel revelation, his comfort, or his efficiency, by a disseverance of all symbolical and special reference to this truth from the significancy of his profession? Is nothing lost to the cause of truth in respect to its practical influence in the world? Is nothing lost with regard to the direct manifestation of the Spirit's influence in His power over the hearts of men?

Our Lord assured His disciples that in "that day," when, having "laid down His life" in "finishing the work which had been given

Him to do," He should return to the Father in the full glory of His resurrection state, it would be their privilege to seek the communications of divine grace *in His name*, in such measure that their "joy should be full."—John 15: 13; 17: 4; 14: 14—21; 16: 24—30. This fullness of joy, it is to be observed, was to be sought in the name of their risen and glorified Savior. Do we appreciate the full import of this condition in its relation to the attainment of the promised blessing? Do we habitually realize that we enjoy the "first fruits of the Spirit," only as our life is hid with Christ in God? that if we live in the possession of the earnest of our inheritance, it is "because He lives?" Do we seek the abundant influence of the Spirit, as the gift of His offered sacrifice and His entrance into His glory? See John 7: 39; 16: 7. Are not our conceptions of Christian relationship and of Christian privilege, in too great a degree, essentially the same as they might have been on the supposition that the provisions of the covenant of grace, in respect to the work of Christ's humiliation and exaltation, were yet to be fulfilled? Has not the view of the provisions of the gospel which has led to the exclusion of all symbolical allusion to His resurrection life from the significancy of the Christian profession, too far pervaded and given character to the prevalent conceptions of practical Christianity? And can the largest measures of the Spirit's renewing and sanctifying influence be hoped for while this deficiency continues? It is a perpetual truth that it is the "glory of Christ" which is to be shed forth on those who "believe on Him through the word" of the gospel. It is the power of Christ which, in its abundant sufficiency, is to rest upon them. It is He who is to be recognized as their "life." Can it be doubted that if these conceptions as to the Source and conditions of the Christian life, could generally attain in their relation to the views and experience of the disciples of Christ, the place which is given them in the teaching of the New Testament, influencing and controlling their familiar apprehensions of truth, continually impelling to aspirations after higher degrees of spiritual attainment, and entering spontaneously and irresistably into their whole religious life, it would mark a new era in Christian devotion and enjoyment and efficiency?

And is it nothing that the rite which He has appointed to set forth this aspect of Christianity, should be banished from the church? Is it nothing that the ordinance which was designed, by its expressive significancy, to keep these truths ever in remembrance, should be thrust aside from the place of witness and admonition and instruction to which it was assigned by the ascending Redeemer?

It is true, indeed, the ordinance may be observed with all due regard alike for its inherent form and the essential qualifications of its subjects, and with a general recognition of its significancy, while yet there is but a slight appreciation of the fullness and preciousness of the truth embraced in that significancy, in its relation to the experience and obligation of the subject. The liability is in all respects the same in the observance of the Lord's Supper. In an attempt to make obvious the adaptation of either of these ordinances to fulfill the purpose expressed in its appointment, from facts pertaining to its intrinsic nature, we naturally inquire, What is the legitimate influence of a proper recognition of its significancy in its application to the personal experience and duty of the observant, in cases where the full import of that significancy is brought to bear upon his consciousness and his heart? It is not to be overlooked, of course, that such an influence must be viewed as inseparable from a distinct and obedient recognition on his part, of the authority of the Master in the appointment of the rite.

The emblematical ordinances of the gospel are few and simple and expressive. Their very fewness is adapted to secure distinctness and permanence to the impression resulting from their observance, and, in connection with their simplicity and specialty of design, to be a safeguard against any tendency to a ritual formalism in Christian worship. They not only lead the mind directly and immediately to the great facts and truths of the gospel, but they present these in a light in which they are apprehended as related to the actual, conscious experience and faith of the observant. And as in their relation to him they have no proper significancy apart from this faith and experience, they stand as positive and perpetual witnesses that no proposed substitute for a conscious and obedient reception of the gospel, can possibly avail as an evidence on his part of an interest in the "spiritual blessings in Christ Jesus" which are represented.

Each of these rites occupies, in its connection with a visible Christianity and the recognition and privileges of a visible church membership, precisely the position for which, by its nature and design and import, it is intrinsically, and with most obvious and perfect fitness, adapted. The Lord's Supper, as an ordinance to be observed within the church, is a perpetual remembrancer of the atoning sacrifice of the Author of redemption, and of the continued interest of the recipient in its efficacy. Baptism as occupying a position at the very starting point of a public identification of the subject, in his profession, with Christianity, most appropriately summons attention to the great central facts and truths of the Christian system, as the characteristic objects of his faith, the ground of his hope, and the source of his incentives to the pursuit of a distinctive Christian life, while it is a significant declaration on his part, that, in actual experience, in sympathy, and in purpose, he is, and is henceforth to be, identified with them in their assimilating and controlling influence over his nature. In a more exact view of his relations, it proclaims the fact that he has attained to a living union with Him who is at the same time recognized as the living Object of his faith and Source of all his blessings, in a conscious fellowship with Him in the design of His work of redemption, and the bringing of the soul into vital connection with His resurrection life as the influence by which he is to be animated, sustained, guided, controlled, and finally made perfect in a resurrection with Him in glory. What possible provision could so exactly, so characteristically, so comprehensively, so effectively, exhibit the nature of the truth which is professed, or fasten upon the mind of the subject, in indelible impression, an appreciation of his peculiar relations, obligations and privileges, and of his ground of confidence with regard to "the end of his faith?" Is it possible that an ordinance of such import, of such perfect adaptation to answer the important purposes embraced within its design, and so inseparable from impressions which must naturally be as lasting, as they are salutary, was assigned its position by Him who appointed it, in order that it might be disregarded by His disciples? Was it enjoined that it might be neglected?

There are communities whose members, under the plea of a reliance on the immediate guidance of the Spirit, have entirely discarded the symbolical ordinances of Christianity. They unconditionally set aside both baptism and the Lord's Supper. In this they may be equally indifferent to the loss in spiritual comfort and edification and quickening of Christian feeling, which is thus incurred, as to the practical disregard which is evinced for the appointments of Him in whom they may trust for salvation, and for the witness which through these ordinances He requires of His people "till He come." But shall their indifference to these considerations of privilege and of duty, be accepted by the believer in Christ as his standard of aspiration or rule of action? Does their failure to seek or even to appreciate or to desire the benefits to be received from this source, render these benefits any the less real or important in their relation to the experience of those who have allowed their feelings and decision to be brought into practical sympathy with the wisdom of the Master in the institution of these ordinances? Or, admitting, perhaps, the reality and desirableness of the benefit to be derived from the symbolical observance involved in the celebration of the Lord's Supper, shall we assume that we have no interest in any similar advantage as connected with baptism? Why should the life-long impression resulting from the act of obedience whereby, in its very profession of the gospel, the soul enters, in its faith, its apprehension of truth, its appropriation of motives, in all its holiest sympathies, desires and purposes, *into the significancy of baptism* as a representation of union with Christ in a fellowship with Him in the design of His death and the blessedness of His resurrection life, be regarded as a benefit of less importance than the other? In its realization it is equally a matter of conscious, joyous experience. In its operation it is equally effective in securing a regard for the facts which are represented. And in the extent of its influence it is commensurate with the range and application of the truth which is recognized in such a profession.

Nor is this a benefit to be enjoyed at the sacrifice or hazard of any other. The means by which it is secured, are in no respect a substitute for the reality to which they relate. They present no false or inadequate view of gospel truth or of Christian life. They are no arbitrary provision of mere ecclesiastical origin. They have been established in no spirit of accomodation to the preferences of those by whom they are employed. They are not only in perfect harmony, in their tendency and influence, with every doctrine of revelation, and every aspect of a genuine Christian experience, but they are the very means which the Author of the gospel Himself has ordained for presenting these truths and this experience in their true light, and rendering them in the highest degree effective. As such they are accompanied with an influence which reaches the inmost springs of action in its tendency to bring every thought and aspiration and purpose of the soul into complete sympathy with the truth which is thus emblematically professed. Shall the Christian say that he does not need this influence? that these are benefits which he has no occasion to enjoy? that the means which His Savior has thus graciously provided to enable him to attain the most effectually the end of his calling, may be treated by him with indifference and practical disregard?

But the question urged upon his decision is not simply one which relates to his reception or enjoyment of personal benefits. It is equally one of fidelity in *witnessing* to the truth of the gospel. The symbolical ordinances of Christ's appointment, are in this respect designed to answer each a distinct but analagous purpose. Does the faithful observance of the Lord's Supper subserve an important end in proclaiming to the world the relation of the death of Christ to the remission of sins? Does it contribute directly to the preservation in the church of a distinct and effective recognition of the efficacy and importance of His atoning sacrifice? It is obvious that it does this only as the rite is recognized as retaining its *symbolical significancy*. Do those by whom it is observed, believe that a form introduced as a substitute, which should entirely set aside the requisition respecting the *breaking* of the bread, and the *eating* and *drinking* of the elements, in any literal or proper sense of these terms, and which, omitting all symbolical allusion to the sacrifice of Christ, should seek to supply its place by some emblematical reference to His transfiguration on the mount, or to His deeds of mercy in the exercise of His miraculous power, would sufficiently meet the design of the ordinance? Would it suffice to urge that it is only necessary that we have a rite which shall, in some significant way, remind us of the work of Christ, or of some important event in His history; that a representation of His work in one particular involves by implication a virtual reference to it in every other; that such a transaction may as really be observed in remembrance of Christ, as the rite described in the sacred record; and that it is supposed, of course, that His death in its atoning efficacy, will be within the knowledge and recognition of every observant who is acquainted with the gospel history and the general teaching of the New Testament? Is it difficult to perceive what would be the direct and irresistible *tendency* of such a substitution, and of such a method of vindication, in respect to the specific truth for the representation and proclamation of which the original rite was instituted? How obviously would the observance at every point in its operation prove its essential deficiency to answer the design of the ordinance appointed by our Lord! But the failure could in no respect be more manifest, or the tendency more disastrous, than in the analagous attempt to set aside the symbolical import of baptism.

It may seem needless to remark, that to the perpetuation of the rite it is essential that the act expressed in its enacting term, and with which its very significancy, as explained by the sacred writers, is inherently identified,—Rom. 6: 4; Col. 2: 12,—should be preserved. True it is, as in the case of the Lord's Supper, that not even this could be of any avail except as viewed in its relation to the thing signified; but, as, also, in the one case, so in the other, it is impossible that the thing signified should be properly expressed by a form which has no inherent adaptation to express it.

It is not a matter of indifference that a profession of Christianity should be associated with the use of a form which is regarded as having no natural significancy beyond what is recognized, perhaps, in some general idea of Christian dedication, and which accordingly, whether it be administered in connection with the consciousness of the subject, or received by him in infancy, is claimed to have equally fulfilled its design. Nothing is more natural than to seek the essential import of the profession in the *import of the rite* in which it is made, or by which it is represented. This tendency, even where attempts may be made to guard against it by verbal explanation, is as inevitable and resistless as it is natural. The substitution is more than a simple omission. As far as the act performed has a significancy, it has the effect to *divert* attention from the import of the original rite. It tends to create and perpetuate the impression that the great truth which in reality is characteristic of the whole Christian system, which has the most direct relations to all that is precious and effective in Christian life, is *not* a truth to claim a distinct recognition in a *symbolical profession* of the gospel; that the vital relationship to Christ pertaining to His death and resurrection, which chiefly indicates the nature and end of the Christian's faith and experience and hope, is not of such importance that it should be specifically embraced in the significancy of a rite by which an interest in the blessings of the kingdom of Christ is to be signified.

The natural influence of such a cause continually operating to give shape and direction to the views and thoughts and life of those who are subject to it, needs only to be suggested to be perceived. A sufficient indication of its tendency may, perhaps, be seen in the nature of the considerations which are usually urged in vindication of the usage. Why, for example, is it suggested that the hope which may be entertained with regard to the *future* state of those who are taken away in infancy, or before they have fully known to discern between good and evil, is to be our guide in determining the relationship of the living to the kingdom of Christ? To assume that every individual of the human race upon his birth into the world has the necessary spiritual qualifications for baptism, would be virtually to find the proof that he is "born of the Spirit," in the fact that he is "born of the flesh," and would tend to destroy all motive on his part to "strive to enter in at the strait gate," or to "find the way that leadeth unto life," and all incentive on the part of the church to persuade or induce him to "seek" that he may find. The gospel recognizes the necessity of a *new* birth, a new relationship of life in Christ Jesus; and the only *evidence* to the church, or to any individual of the human family, which can possibly indicate its existence, is *faith*. Hence faith is an essential prerequisite to its recognition in baptism.—Col. 2: 12.

Baptism as a representation of a vital union with Christ in the likeness of His death and resurrection, is a witness that the Christian's relationship is essentially and radically *different* from the national relationship of the Jewish commonwealth. It does not exist by virtue of natural descent or a connection with parents. It is not the result of any simple dedication. It is, as connected with a "new covenant," which is "established upon better promises," and of which the Mediator "ever lives to make intercession," the relationship of a NEW LIFE,—of a new life on the part of such as being "by nature" "dead in sins," are, by the power of God, quickened together with Christ, and raised up together, and made to sit together in heavenly places in Him, through *the faith* of the operation of God, who raised Him from the dead.

In the reception and possession of this life is the world's only hope. To reveal it,—in its reality, its source, its conditions, the way in which it is to be obtained, its requisitions, the nature and method of its operation, its present fruits, and its final consummation, is, as connected with the manifestation of the divine glory, the design of the gospel. It is to it, as to a more ultimate end, that the forgiveness of sins by the sacrifice of Christ, has reference. In the full enjoyment of it must be found the health and efficiency of the church. Is the prevalent standard of Christian attainment and action such as to indicate that there is no hindrance to the operation of its appropriate influence? Is it to take no deeper and firmer hold on the Christian consciousness? Are the people of God generally to attain to no higher appreciation of the things revealed in His word pertaining to the provision for their redemption? or of their own privileges and responsibility as those who "in Christ" are "alive from the dead?" Is the power of prayer to have no additional illustration in their experience? Has the fruit of the Spirit, which is "in all goodness and righteousness and truth," already attained its fullest development in their life and character? Is the law of benevolence to find no broader and more complete application in connection with their selfdenying labors in behalf of the needy and the sinful? Must the nations of the earth for generations to come be abandoned to the darkness and guilt of their apostacy from God? Shall the millions at our own doors who are the proper objects of our compassion, be left still to pass on in their ignorance and degradation and sin, with no more earnest efforts to secure to them the means and influences by which they may attain the true end of their being?

Is it asked, How is this more perfect realization of the object of the Christian life, so essential to the full development in the disciples of Christ of the spirit and power of Christianity, and so closely connected with all that concerns the welfare of the world that lies in wickedness, to be attained? We may not, as guided by the teaching of the divine word, overlook the fact, that, as related to the operation of the Spirit of God, the appropriate influence for attaining it must be sought in connection with a proper appreciation of *the facts and truths and relations* which are exhibited in the significancy of baptism as the representative rite of the Christian profession. It may scarcely be necessary to remark, that the baptism itself is but the appointed provision for the acknowledgement of the Christian's interest in these realities, for bringing them into their proper connection with his profession and life, and for securing to them their full effect as they may be recognized in their relation to his experience and obligation. The profession cannot fulfill its design apart from a suitable appreciation of its import. The mind must enter into the significance and spirit of the truth professed, and yield to it the most hearty assent in its application to whatever pertains to Christian privilege and responsibility. But, on the other hand, it is not to be inferred that this truth may be dissevered from all specific relation to such a profession, and yet suffer no disadvantage as to its position for exerting the most effectually its proper influence. The considerations which may be urged to show that the doctrine of Christ's death and resurrection in their reality and effects, as presented in such passages as Rom. 6: 1—14; 8: 11—34; Col. 2: 12, 20: 3: 1—4, etc., has no *special* relation to a symbolical profession of the gospel, may be not less adapted to nurture the impression that it has no *special* relation to the Christian life which is to follow that profession. The same state of mind which would insist that it should have no distinct or prominent recognition in the significancy of a rite which marks a separation from the world, may easily fail to give it any distinct or prominent position in its relation to the separation itself. If it be really and distinctly recognized as occupying such a position with respect to the latter, why should it be refused a corresponding expression in connection with the former? Why should not the sign be allowed to answer in this particular to the thing signified? In the former case, no less than in the latter, the explicit teaching of the word of inspiration, must be accepted as the only safe or admissable rule of faith or of action.

Our Lord in associating baptism, in inseparable connection, with the "preaching of the gospel" and with "faith," in His final commission, most clearly intended to indicate its importance as a means for accomplishing the great purposes of His kingdom. It was placed in that connection, not that the words might be read in the public assembly, or in the retirement of the family, and dismissed without further regard or attention. It was designed that the ordinance, thus presented and enjoined, should exert a life-long influence in its relation to a recognition of the truth to be "preached" and "believed." The same Spirit of inspiration that teaches that there is "one Lord" and "one faith," declares in the same sentence, and with equal apparent emphasis, that there is also "one baptism." It is such in its importance, not as an external observance and a profession merely, but as an observance and a profession which are a medium through which the great truths of the gospel are to be permanently effective in their relation to the exemplification of the "faith" professed,—whereby their distinctive features may become, in a manner, daguerreotyped upon the Christian's consciousness, ever recalling to his recognition their relation to his experience and life, and their claims to his regard and obedience.

It is through the significancy of their profession in baptism, that the disciples of Christ are to be continually reminded, that they have entered into the efficacy of His vicarious death, not simply to receive its full benefit for the forgiveness of their sins, but in order that they may be perpetually subject to its assimilating power with reference to the destruction of sin in their nature;— that they are in their essential relationship and experience, as they should be in all their cherished feelings and aims and purposes, "dead with Christ" to the service of sin, so that it may not have dominion over them,—dead with Him to the "rudiments of the world," as supplying any possible expedient for their justification,— dead with Him to "things on the earth," as objects on which to set their affection, or which may give direction to their aspirations or pursuits. The recollection of their profession is also continually to recall to their minds, invested with ever fresh interest, the other great fact in their experience, to wit, that, as they have entered into the fellowship of the death of Christ, so have they "risen with Him" to the enjoyment of a new, spiritual life and a new relationship of adoption in Him;—that, as partakers of the infinite merit of His accepted sacrifice and "the power of His resurrection," it is for them to rest in Him as their unfailing ground of hope and source of perpetual peace and strength and joy;—that their life, as hid with Him in God, is not of this world, and that consequently they are to seek those things which are above, where He sits on the right hand of God, and to be continually aspiring to the perfection of their life with Him in glory. While they live under the controlling influence of these conceptions of their relation and privileges, these desires and aspirations and purposes, it will be impossible that the world should fill their minds or absorb their energies. Earthly objects will by them be esteemed valuable only as viewed in their relation to Christ,—it will be alike their constant aim and their highest joy, to live, not to themselves, but to Him, as one who is recognized as having "died for them and risen again." Nor should it escape attention that they will thus be in the most effective connection and living sympathy with the truth which is represented in the *name* of Him through whom is ever to be sought the abundant communication of the Spirit.

Is it said that the recognition and effect of these truths are not necessarily dependent upon their connection with the profession with which they thus appear in the representation of the New Testament, to be associated? We ask, why should they be dissevered from this connection? It will hardly be claimed that there is any other method so natural and direct by which they may be effective to the results which have been indicated. And who can adequately estimate what may be lost by an unnatural "sundering" of that which Christ, in His infinite wisdom, has thus "joined together" in the order of His kingdom? Is not a *profession* of the truth an essential feature in the divine arrangement for securing the full design of its revelation? Was it not revealed that it might be professed, as well as enjoyed? And can any transaction sufficiently answer the purpose of such a profession, which does not present that truth in its Scriptural aspects and relations? Are those who may the most lightly esteem the benefits to be received from a personal relation to the significancy of baptism and the Lord's Supper, entirely confident that the devout and earnest observance of these ordinances, as they appear in the New Testament in connection with the practice of the primitive Christians, would not bring, even to themselves, some important additional advantages? It is doubtless true that the neglect of the rite of profession appointed by our Lord, results chiefly from a failure adequately to appreciate the importance and application of the doctrinal and practical truth which it represents. Let the Christian in making a profession of the gospel, have a proper conception of the relation of this profession as made in baptism, to the death and resurrection of Christ,—let him apprehend fully, as is explained in the apostolic epistles, that through his identification with the rite, he is to be known and recognized as united to Christ "in the likeness of His death and resurrection,"—let him, in the grateful feelings and purposes of his soul, enter truly into the *spirit* of the requisition that, as a public declaration of his relationship to Christ, he be "buried with Him in baptism," and the act of obedience in this respect will follow as naturally as it did in the case of the Christians at Rome or Colosse.

The significancy which our Lord has identified with baptism, is not a mere form. The truth which it represents, and as represented, is not a form. The relationship and experience which it symbolizes, are not a form. In these in their connection with a proper profession of Christianity, are involved obligations and interests which no disciple of the Lord Jesus Christ may regard with lightness or inattention. The same wisdom which in the promulgation of the word of truth, has indicated what shall be *believed*, has prescribed with equal explicitness what shall be significantly *professed*. The same authority which has appointed the ordinance of the Supper, and made it the sign of a continued participation in the efficacy of the atoning sacrifice of the gospel, has determined and established both the rite and the *significancy* of baptism, and has made it the symbol of a living union with Christ in a conscious fellowship with Him in His death and resurrection. Is the authority in the latter case, less decisive or imperative, than in the former? Is the truth to be proclaimed less important? Nay, as it is characteristic of the very profession of the gospel, and extends over the whole range of Christian relationship and duty, is not its importance in some respects peculiar?

In the significancy of baptism we have the characteristic insignia of the "banner" which God has given to His people, "that it may be displayed because of the truth." It is only as the distinctive truth which by His own hand He has inscribed on this sign of the Christian faith and the Christian life, shall be properly recognized by them, and, being thus recognized, shall be so regarded that it may become thoroughly effective upon their hearts and lives, that they will be prepared to go forth to the conquest of the world. Who can calculate the full measure of the responsibility involved in an attempt on their part to efface from the Christian profession this divine inscription? It was written there by the Captain of their salvation for the most important purposes relating to the interests of the cause of truth and the welfare of the souls of men. It was written there that, being accepted by them as the sign of their union with Him, it might be kept ever before their eye, inspiring their faith and hope and courage, animating their zeal and devotion, while it should proclaim to the world,—"I am He that liveth, and was dead; and, behold, I am alive for evermore, Amen; and have the keys of hell and of death." It was written there that its meaning might be associated with their most familiar thoughts of duty and purposes of action, continually assuring them that "if they be dead with Christ, they shall also live with Him," and that in the "gospel" which proclaims His vicarious *death* and His glorious *resurrection*, with their connected results, they may find the most effective motives to be "steadfast, unmovable, always abounding in the work of the Lord."

BAPTISMAL HARMONIES.

(SEE TITLE PAGE.)

THE book will contain some twenty-five or more baptismal metrical hymns by the author of the volume, besides the selections of Scriptural passages and compositions for chanting, and the hymns on the Lord's Supper and the Christian Sabbath. The number of pages in the book will be not less than *ninety-six*, fifty of which will be original music.

The volume has been prepared with reference to the attainment of three distinct but closely related objects.

I. As a book of instruction and persuasive appeal FOR GENERAL CIRCULATION, it properly consists of three parts:

1. The baptismal metrical HYMNS, each designed to meet some special purpose in its relation to the doctrine of baptism, and each complete in itself, will be found to cover the whole ground of Scriptural teaching with reference to the Christian rite, in its more important doctrinal, historical and practical relations. Truth expressed in the form of *lyric poetry*, has a tendency to gain a lodgement in the memory and the heart, in many cases where all other modes of presenting it fail of the end. And the query may well be suggested, whether this method of "teaching" the Gospel, has been sufficiently appreciated by the churches in their missionary and other efforts to fulfill the great commission.

2. Each of the hymns is preceded, on the same page, by a series of SCRIPTURAL PASSAGES and references, presenting, in their import and arrangement, a suggestive argument and appeal with regard to the subject matter of the hymn, and the whole, as arranged on the successive pages, furnishing a very complete *Scriptural Guide* upon the various important doctrines which are directly related to baptism. In this respect, it is hoped the book will be found useful in the hands of the young Christian and of the inquirer, as well as of those of more mature experience.

3. The hymns and quotations from the Scriptures are preceded by an INTRODUCTION of eight pages, which constitutes in itself a sort of distinct treatise upon the *nature and importance of the truth* professed and represented in baptism, especially as it stands related, both doctrinally and experimentally, to those great central facts of Christianity, the vicarious *death* and *resurrection life* of Christ, and illustrating the *natural significance* and *importance* of baptism as a profession of this truth and a memorial of these facts.

II. As a HYMN BOOK FOR DEVOTIONAL PURPOSES, it is designed chiefly to answer a two-fold purpose:

1. To furnish a sufficient variety of hymns setting forth the design and relations of baptism, and appealing appropriately to the experience of the candidates and the church, as also to the spectators, to meet the natural demands of *baptismal occasions*.

2. To supply hymns relating to the doctrine of baptism, which may, with good effect, be used on ordinary occasions of public and social worship.

III. As a MUSIC BOOK, containing some fifty pages of new music, it is designed—

1. To supply appropriate tunes for giving expression to the sentiment of the hymns as sung on baptismal and other occasions.

2. To furnish, in connection with its uses as a Hymn Book, what, it is believed, is entirely wanting in the music books in common use—a variety of *baptismal chants and anthems*—the former arranged chiefly with appropriate selections of Scriptural passages.

3. To aid in introducing into choirs and churches, a variety of excellent tunes, which it is not doubted will be found exceedingly acceptable for ordinary purposes of public and social worship. The value of a really good tune, brought into general use, in promoting devotional feeling, and imparting interest to devotional exercises, cannot easily be estimated. Eph. 5: 19.

www.ingramcontent.com/pod-product-compliance
Lightning Source LLC
Chambersburg PA
CBHW020127170426
43199CB00009B/673